Narcissistic Abuse Recovery

A New Life of Beauty & Peace for the HSP: How the Highly Sensitive Person Practices Mindfulness, Self-Love and Core Values to Set Boundaries and Make Healthy Relationships

Loralee Jean

©Copyright 2022 by Loralee Jean - All rights reserved.

The content contained within this book may not be reproduced, duplicated or transmitted without direct written permission from the author or the publisher.

Under no circumstances will any blame or legal responsibility be held against the publisher, or author, for any damages, reparation, or monetary loss due to the information contained within this book. Either directly or indirectly. You are responsible for your own choices, actions, and results.

Legal Notice:

This book is copyright protected. This book is only for personal use. You cannot amend, distribute, sell, use, quote or paraphrase any part, or the content within this book, without the consent of the author or publisher.

Disclaimer Notice:

Please note the information contained within this document is for educational and entertainment purposes only. All effort has been executed to present accurate, up-to-date, and reliable, complete information. No warranties of any kind are declared or implied. Readers acknowledge that the author is not engaging in the
rendering of legal, financial, medical or professional advice. The content within this book has been derived from various sources. Please consult a licensed professional before attempting any techniques outlined in this book.

By reading this document, the reader agrees that under no circumstances is the author responsible for any losses, direct or indirect, which are incurred as a result of the use of the information contained within this document, including, but not limited to, — errors, omissions, or inaccuracies.

Contents

My Gift To You	V
Introduction	1
Part One: Celebrate Your Nature	7
1. The Distinguishable Traits of Being Highly Sensitive	9
2. The Destructive Bond Between HSPs and Narcissists	25
3. Understand and Celebrate Your Personality	39
Part Two: Cultivate Healing Habits	53
4. The Mindset for Starting Over	55
5. Introverted Healing Habits	69
6. Extroverted Healing Habits	91
Part Three: Curate Good Relationships	109

7. Cull Connections and Recognize Toxicity	111
8. Make New Friends and Recognize Healthy Love	125
Part Four: Custodian Sacred Spaces	139
9. Your Need for a Safe Space	141
10. Building Boundaries for Others	153
11. Holding Space for Yourself	165
Part Five: Clear The Clutter	175
12. Simplicity and Slowness in Physical Spaces	177
Final Words	191
Afterword	197
Leave a Review!	199
Join A Supportive Community!	201
My Gift to You	202
References	204

My Gift To You

Hello Lovely!

I have put together a 33-page companion workbook to go along with the many practical strategies described in *Narcissistic Abuse Recovery*. Grab your free PDF copy, print it out and refer to it as you continue reading. I think it will be a great additional resource for your healing journey!

Grab it here!
freebie.myrecoveryyear.com

Cheers to your recovery!

Loralee Jean

Grab it here!
freebie.myrecoveryyear.com

Introduction

The world was both beautiful and terrifying for a young woman named Tabitha. It held such passion and emotion, and she could find something significant and compelling in even the most minor thing. She felt love keenly as she did every other enjoyable emotion. And yet, there was a price to pay. Just as passionately, she felt anger and sadness with severity. Disappointment reigned heavy inside her, as did resentment and fear. She loved exuberantly with everything in her and was open to finding happiness in each moment. Yet, at the same time, she also noticed negative things when they did arise. And she did so sooner than others. Tabitha wanted to give to others, but there was also a limit. She needed time on her own to replenish her energy. Busy places, loud situations, and stressful times drained that energy from her, making her feel weak and tired. Her nature made her observant, compassionate, and loving. Still, it also sometimes made her feel fragile, frightened and taken advantage of by others.

Enter Derrick. At first, he'd thought the world of Tabitha, at least telling her so, and together they began a new life. Tabitha saw his softer side and how he had experienced trauma in life, and she wanted to give, give, give. But Derrick saw an opportunity to take advantage of a loving and generous heart. With every passing year, he took more and more, creating unfair expectations of Tabitha, always centred around him and his needs. Their marriage suffered severely, and in the end, they parted ways, Tabitha feeling more broken, in pain, and confused than ever before.

I've been there. I know Tabitha's pain and her constant battle with the world. I, too, know what it's like to have a marriage where you initially feel like the other person completely understands and adores you. In the end, however, you're left empty and drained of all passion for life. I am a highly sensitive person, a term coined by psychologist Elaine Aron in her book, *The Highly Sensitive Person* (Jarai, 2022). It means that I (and Tabitha!) look at the world differently, and while it can be a benefit in so many ways, it can also be a hindrance.

Sadly, many people with the capacity for deep love and care find themselves in dangerous and abusive relationships. Unfortunately, they often make prime candidates for these kinds of relationships. We'll learn more about HSPs together, and overall, I want us to focus on the highly sensitive person's recovery from narcissistic abuse. In my case, I was married to a covert narcissist for five years. I dealt with emotional abuse, depression, and being a victim. In the relationship, I did not find the love and support I needed, so I went through cycles of anxiety, depression, and feelings of worthlessness.

But now, I've found freedom from that pain through study, hard work, and determination to pursue an authentic and bold life. As a single mom, I want to exemplify strength, self-love and compassion to my children. So, I decided to rebuild my life from the ground up, to live a healthier and happier, more fulfilling life than I had previously known. Instead of tripping over my attributes of high sensitivity, I intentionally worked to understand my nature and flow with it instead of letting my sensitivities overpower my life.

That's what I want to do with you. If you see yourself in my or Tabitha's story or believe you're a highly sensitive person who finds the world frustrating yet deeply meaningful, and if you have had trouble with relationships, this is just the right book for you. I want to help you appreciate, celebrate, and nurture the aspects of your highly sensitive personality. I want to help you be mindful of the relationships you choose to foster in your life and learn the confidence and strength to get out of relationships that no longer serve you. I want to help you find and use your voice.

During my time in an abusive relationship, I felt like I had no voice and no one to speak for me. So I had to learn to speak for myself and find a new, healthier path. It was up to me to pioneer my healing journey, and now I want to empower you to do the same.

With the tools discussed in this book, you can educate yourself about your highly sensitive personality and learn all the beauty and power found in the attributes you have. You will also understand why HSPs and narcissists often find each other, and we'll discuss healthy habits to cope with the aftermath of narcissistic abuse. My other goals are that you learn how to cultivate happy, healthy relationships that bring you support, love, and joy. Holding it all together, we'll discuss building boundaries that keep you safe from future abuse. I also want you to find your sacred space, the inner place where you can appreciate your uniqueness as a highly sensitive person. As you recover from narcissistic abuse, I want to return you to yourself, so you'll connect with and believe in yourself and all you have to offer. Finally, we'll discuss simplicity and the power of slowing down.

INTRODUCTION 5

Life should be enjoyed, not endured; this can be tough to remember for an HSP. There is so much around us that threatens to steal our joy. But I'm here to tell you that I have found a pathway to healing in my life after emotional abuse. It may seem out of reach for you right now, but it **is** possible. We highly sensitive people may see the world differently, but we have gifts and skills others do not have. These gifts and abilities can give us a more profound, passionate, and beautiful life experience.

Join me on this journey and consider sharing this book with others who will find it beneficial. Find your voice, and empower yourself to chase after the beautiful life you deserve.

Part One: Celebrate Your Nature

The Distinguishable Traits of Being Highly Sensitive

YOU MIGHT NOT HAVE known about this term, even if you are highly sensitive. However, it's come around relatively recently, and, finally, people who were constantly being told they were "too sensitive," "weak," or "awkward" have something positive to be. They finally have a term that identifies who they are; it isn't inadequate or useless; it is merely a descriptive fact of their nature. Not only that, but the traits that accompany a highly sensitive person are special and unique, and even if it makes life a little bit more challenging to get through at times, these traits can bring strength and power to the HSP, distinguishing them entirely from the rest of the world.

Intro to the Science Behind It

The intent of this book is not to be overly scientific; still, the more you know about your highly sensitive personality, the better you can understand yourself and how you interact with others. You can learn to avoid pitfalls that can get you into sticky situations and pursue those situations which showcase your strengths.

As I mentioned in the introduction, psychologist Elaine Aron is the one who titled this term. *Highly sensitive* refers to people who are more reactive to stimuli than others. Aron believes that 15-20 percent of the population is highly sensitive (Jarai, 2022).

Alane Freud, a Licensed Marriage and Family Therapist and close friend and colleague of Elaine Aron, explains that the trait of high sensitivity is also found in 15-20 percent of over 100 species and has a clear evolutionary benefit. The research in animal species shows two distinct behavioural strategies. In 80-85 percent of certain species, the creature has an impulsive, go-for-it demeanour in which they just try something, and if it doesn't go well, they just try again. In primates, this trait was classified as "laidback." The other 15-20 percent have a "do it right and do it once" attitude, demonstrating a responsive, reflective and reactive nature. This is the high-sensitivity trait; in primates, it was classified as "uptight."

In a pond filled with Pumpkinseed Sunfish, biologists at Cornell University in New York observed the fish's reaction to a new trap placed in the water. They found that most of the Pumpkinseed Sunfish were bold, swam right in, and were trapped. But a small group of timid fish recognized the novelty of the trap and hesitated, keeping their distance from it and would not enter.

In the presence of food, scientists have observed that fruit flies will either sit or rove about. The sitting flies were shown to have more neuro-complexity. Translation: these highly sensitive flies were thinking more before they went to the food! (Freund, 2019).

While in the past, being highly sensitive might have appeared to others as a weakness or a sign of a mental disorder, an article in *Medical News Today* describes it as an evolved personality trait that can make adaptations (Jarai, 2022). It can be extremely beneficial in your life and relationships to be an HSP, but in reality, people often focus more on its disadvantages and the negative aspects of how it sets you apart from others.

But how do you know if you're an HSP? Consider some of the following questions. (Jarai, 2022)

Do I notice subtle differences in things? Whether tangible or intangible?

Do I process environmental stimuli more deeply?

Do I feel emotions more deeply or keenly? (Especially to supposedly minor events or situations?)

Do I have stronger emotional, physical, or psychological reactions to events?

Do I have a low tolerance for pain?

Do I have a low tolerance for too many stimuli in my environment?

Do I feel significantly affected by other people's moods?

Do I need a lot more alone time than others? (Especially as a way to recharge or reenergize?)

Do I easily become overwhelmed in high stimuli situations?

Essentially, you could think of an HSP as someone who sees and feels more deeply than others might. While a wild, crowded music concert may feel like heaven to one person, to an HSP, it might feel like hell. The loud noise, the crowding of people, and the thousands upon thousands of voices, expressions, and tones, can overwhelm an HSP to the point where they might want to run away and hide in a corner until they can go home.

If you are still wondering if you're an HSP, imagine yourself in these kinds of high-stimuli situations and think about how you might react:

- an angry confrontation with a friend
- a circus
- a rock concert
- a day-long conference
- a night out with friends
- a holiday party

Would you become stressed, overstimulated, or feel the need to spend time alone to recover from the energy loss you experienced? The more times you answered yes to these questions, the more likely you're an HSP.

The DOES Acronym

To give you an even better understanding of the distinguishable traits of an HSP, use the DOES acronym. Created by Aron in her book, this acronym puts it all together. (Jane, n.d.)

Depth of Processing: HSPs spend more time in reflection than others. Maybe that means they take longer to make decisions or mull over a difficult situation. An HSP's reaction to the world can be conscious or unconscious, such as a gut feeling.

Overarousability: An HSP notices things more efficiently, subtle things, which others might miss. It can be like an extraordinary, secret power or overwhelm the HSP to the extent that they just want to get out.

Emotional Intensity or Empathy: Empathy is an excellent skill of HSPs. They feel so strongly that they can quickly identify with others and feel their pain. But it can also mean HSPs are constantly riding on a roller coaster of other people's emotions, leaving them very drained.

Sensory Sensitivity: An HSP might have physical sensitivities that others do not, like food sensitivity or a heightened sense of smell. They might be irritated by the feel of a particular fabric. It could also be a sensitivity to loud sounds or the visual clutter in a room. Whatever it is, it can be detrimental if not controlled and worked to its advantage.

To better understand a highly sensitive person versus other similar traits/disorders, I want to go through and discuss the differences between other diagnoses people might consider as the reasons for your highly sensitive nature.

HSP Versus Introversion: What's the Difference?

People often equate being highly sensitive with being introverted. But they're not the same. All HSPs will share and exhibit the traits in the DOES acronym, but they will not all react similarly to the same situation. That makes sense. Even if we're all HSPs, it doesn't mean we can always be thrown together into the same category. An HSP might also be an introvert. You can see how they share similar attributes, shying away from overwhelming situations and getting energy from being with themselves instead of others.

But what about the highly sensitive **extrovert**? Sounds impossible, right? Not so. Even though they are not as common as introverts among the highly sensitive, they do, in fact, exist! A highly sensitive extrovert, or HSE, may look something like this:

- Needing time in the inner world but also time with the outer world. An HSE's time in the inner world can be very beneficial, but if one spends too much time there, they can become tired, lethargic, and lacklustre.

- Being very interactive with others when in social situations. They take joy from this interaction.

- Taking time to engage in activities outside the home. These are controlled, chosen by the HSE as something they enjoy, and maybe only done with one or two other people.

- Feeling passionate about subjects they care about and also doing something about it; many times HSEs are social justice activists.

- Having not a lot of trouble making and keeping various friends.

- Loving working with others and creating deep and meaningful connections.

Even so, an HSE will have similar attributes as an HSI (highly sensitive introvert), such as reacting to environmental stimuli. Still, they will not always shy away or need to spend as much time alone as the highly sensitive introvert.

What About Sensory Processing Disorder (SPD)?

Remember, many people might want to classify sensory processing sensitivity (the trait HSPs have) as a disorder because of how it is experienced or perceived as a weakness, but that's not the case. Being highly sensitive is similar to Sensory Processing Disorder, but in this crucial way, they are different: SPD is a neurological disorder, while being an HSP is a biological trait.

Those affected by SPD are on a spectrum (another similarity to HSPs), so depending on the sense that's been altered or hindered in the person, they may have a different reaction to the world.

In an article titled, *Highly Sensitive? Or Sensory Processing Disorder?* (Maureen, n.d.), Sensory Processing Disorder can be classified in these ways:

- a disconnect between the brain and information needed for stimuli processing, so the stimuli might not get processed correctly

- there may be an under-responsiveness to stimuli (may not notice things like sitting in something wet)

- may crave sensory stimuli and enjoy things like loud music, vigorous play, busy places

- there may be over-responsiveness to stimuli

- if that's the case, they will avoid sensory stimulation and get overwhelmed easily

- SPD could also affect movement, fine motor skills, etc.

But as I said, an HSP is different. It is not a disorder but more like a trait about themselves. So despite all the attributes of an HSP, like getting overwhelmed or seeing subtle differences, they can still function healthily in the world. This may not be the case for a person with SPD.

The Differences Between Autism and HSP

Some may wonder if they land on the autism spectrum because of how overstimulated they feel. While there are some similarities, these are also different psychological terms. The difference, similar to SPD, relates to sensory processing. Technically, both autism and high sensitivity are examples of neurodivergence; however, autism is a neurodevelopmental divergence that is either present in someone or not.

But for highly sensitive individuals, the heightened sensitivity lends itself to heightened experiences and interactions (Samson, 2021). Their sensitivities do not affect an HSP's ability to function "normally" or productively. It is a hindrance in some ways, but not in a way that would classify it as a disorder.

The Common Comparison: Empath vs. HSP

One of the most common comparisons to the highly sensitive person is the empath. And it makes sense because they are very similar, but there are a few slight differences. An empath is someone who, like an HSP:

- feels emotions keenly

- wants to give and care for others
- feels the pain of others
- very skilled at empathy (go figure!)

If you know what a narcissist is (we'll get into that later), a narcissist is on the opposite end of the spectrum from an empath. An empath understands and feels emotions very deeply, whereas a narcissist does not have that ability.

In the above list, you can see where an HSP is very similar to an empath. That awesome and deep feeling of emotion and pain and general sensitivity are all the same between these two. An empath has all the characteristics of an HSP, but they take their sensitivities to the next level. They feel subtle energy even stronger than HSPs. Empaths can absorb the energy sensed from their environment and experience it physically. They will take the energy and internalize it, whether negative or positive. It's even more of an immersive experience in the world than what an HSP knows.

Consider the empathic spectrum to look something like this: On the far right end, you have empaths, then, moving left, you have highly sensitive people, then loving, sensitive, caring people, then further down on the far left end, narcissists, and psychopaths, sociopaths, and those who struggle with the human ability to feel empathy for others. One thing to note, though, is that empaths and highly sensitive people are not mutually exclusive. You can also be both. Just imagine the rich world of understanding emotion that would be! (Orloff, 2017).

Are You Highly Sensitive?

Now that we've learned more about HSPs and their attributes, let's dig a little deeper. Do you relate to an HSP? Could you identify yourself as one? Next, let's look at some more attributes about HSPs to help you further determine if you are one or not. Ask yourself these questions (Granneman, 2017):

Do I abhor and turn away from violence or cruelty? This could mean not being able to view violent scenes in shows or movies or even read about cruelty in a book or news article.

Do I have trouble letting things go? Even if something is damaging and needs to be left behind, this can be difficult for HSPs. Hence, the common issue of narcissists getting into relationships with empaths and HSPs.

Do I often do worse at something I know how to do if someone is watching me?

Am I jumpy? Do I easily startle if someone surprises me or I hear a sudden loud noise? This happens because the nervous system is always on high alert, anticipating something to happen.

Do I cry easily? This can be a telltale identifier for HSPs. Not that other people do not cry, but an HSP's emotional well is so full that it easily overflows, and they are moved to tears.

Conclusion

Unfortunately, many wish to take advantage of the gifts and skills of the highly sensitive person, like Derrick with Tabitha. He wanted to take what she could give him without the responsibility of replenishing what she needed. I have spent far too much of my life dimming my light so that others could shine. But when I began my healing, I started to learn about the beautiful strengths of being an HSP. Learning those strengths helped me gain enough confidence to take the necessary steps in my life to recover my independence and freedom.

Even though the HSP looks and acts differently than many others in the world, there are still so many beautiful strengths you can learn to hone. Throughout this book, I hope to emphasize those strengths and help you realize and eventually apply them in your life.

To get you started, check out these fantastic strengths of HSPs, which will bring to the surface the confidence you already had deep inside yourself. Time to wake it up.

Highly sensitive people can...

- Pick up on social cues and subtle social problems. This helps us develop solid and useful social skills!

- Feel great empathy. Empathy lets us look into others and understand what they are going through. This positive attribute makes us strong leaders or managers, and it also gives us the ability to be wonderful friends and partners!

- Detect environmental cues or are sensitive to environmental surroundings. This can help us to detect changes in the environment or even potential dangers!

Summary

This chapter covered the basic concepts of highly sensitive people. It also covered:

- the science behind highly sensitive people
- the attributes that make up HSPs

- the differences between HSPs and other psychologically altered behaviours.

The next chapter will delve into the relationship issues between HSPs and narcissists. I'll cover why HSPs are more common victims of this type of abuse. At the same time, I'll provide you with ways to recover and get out of narcissistically abusive relationships. There is always hope!

The Destructive Bond Between HSPs and Narcissists

SADLY, BECAUSE OF THE attributes of an HSP, they are very commonly vulnerable to narcissistic abuse. Since we notice things others might not see, we are good at being friends and partners, thinking of others and doing and saying small things to make the other person happy. We also feel emotions intensely, and when getting together with the narcissist, we may discover someone else who engages in intense emotions and behaviours. At first, that's exciting, but then it becomes an issue. Derrick found that Tabitha could meet the needs he wanted to be fulfilled, and for a little while, Derrick gave Tabitha what she wanted. But then, everything changed.

A relationship between a narcissist and anyone will be destructive and dangerous, with the non-narcissistic partner feeling unloved and unsupported. But it's far worse for the HSP because they tend to experience profound emotions. And because we can so quickly feel the emotions and subtle changes in others, we start to lose our connection to ourselves in a relationship with a narcissist. We become so wrapped up in another's emotions that we forget the importance of our own. In this chapter, I'll focus on what a narcissist is, how they operate, and the unfortunate destructive dynamic between HSPs and narcissists. But don't worry. There is always hope for recovery after getting out of an abusive relationship.

What is a Narcissist?

A narcissist is someone who has Narcissistic Personality Disorder. Most of us have experienced a narcissist in one way or another, and you might easily recognize the narcissist in your life through these attribute descriptions. (Miller, n.d.)

A narcissist...

Has a great need for admiration and will do whatever it takes to get it.

Has a lack of empathy and an actual inability to care about/understand others' emotions.

Has a sense of self-importance that makes them believe they are better than others.

Will look down on others whom they think are lower than them in some way.

Exaggerates their achievements and skills in such a way that they begin to believe them.

Expect favours and gifts from others without actually having to do anything that would earn them those things.

Exploits the weaknesses of others to get what they want.

Has grandiose ideas about their future success.

Is envious of others and believes everyone else is jealous of them too.

Behaves arrogantly.

Wants to be connected with high-status people.

Needs to have the best of everything.

Has deep insecurity issues they need to fill through these behaviours.

Even though these sound like very flagrant and easy-to-spot behaviours, that isn't always the case. The narcissist may not show others this side of themselves until they've secured a friendship or a romantic relationship. Many times narcissists are very outgoing, charming, and attractive people. Hence the reason they are still able to get into relationships, despite their personality disorder.

There is a spectrum of narcissism, which can look different from person to person; however, it is important to recognize these two distinct expressions: grandiose narcissists and vulnerable narcissists. With this knowledge at your disposal, you'll be readily able to spot a narcissist when they come across your path.

A grandiose narcissist is the one you are likely to think of when you hear the term *narcissist*. They are usually extroverted types with exaggerated, apparent ways of demonstrating narcissism. They have a superiority complex, and they are arrogant and entitled. They demand attention and praise, think they're better than everyone else, and carry a sense of entitlement to special treatment.

A vulnerable narcissist wants the same adoration and attention as the grandiose narcissist, but their method for bleeding it out of a person differs and may be difficult to spot. They are still self-absorbed and believe in their entitlement; however, these narcissists are more reactive to even gentle criticism and need constant reinforcement. You might find that these narcissists play the victim card over and over again when in fact, they are the ones trying to gain control. Unlike the grandiose narcissist, the vulnerable one will be more introverted and may even shy away from people to avoid the terrible criticism they are so afraid of (Brogaard, 2019).

The HSP and the Narcissist in a Romance

Even though an HSP can spot things others might miss, they are just as easily duped by this kind of charming, attractive person. Anyone who appears confident, assured, fun, and successful will be attractive to others. A narcissist gets very good at hiding the darker aspects of themselves. This is very true, especially at the beginning, when they are trying to secure a relationship with a highly sensitive person.

Love-Bombing

The telltale sign of a narcissist in a romantic relationship is love-bombing. Love-bombing is an intense time at the start of a relationship where you feel completely loved, adored, and appreciated for the special person you are. Love-bombing is more than just the honeymoon phase. You feel loved in a way that is completely catered to you. HSPs value connection and communication, so the narcissist will behave in a way that makes you feel very close and attracted even during this early stage.

Love-bombing "covers over a multitude of sins." You, as the HSP, feel the deep, meaningful connection you are always searching for in relationships. Because HSPs often don't feel appreciated or loved for who they are, the narcissist exploits that fact. This newfound relationship might be the first time the HSP has ever experienced feeling seen and understood, and it creates a sturdy romantic bond on the side of the highly sensitive person. And remember, HSPs are all about those dynamic emotions, so they will enjoy the intensity even more than a non-HSP.

But then, after a certain amount of time, the narcissist will realize they've done the work of securing the relationship and will start to bring out their other side. (Miller, n.d.)

When the Narcissist Retreats

Without fail, the narcissist will always retreat once the relationship is secured. It will happen suddenly because the narcissist has only been pretending to care deeply about the HSP. The abrupt shift in the relationship gives the narcissist an even tighter grip on the highly sensitive person. I first noticed this shift on my honeymoon, immediately after the narcissist secured my relationship with the formal covenant of marriage.

Instantly, the HSP will hurry to fix the relationship. They will wonder what they did wrong and try to figure out what they did to cause the narcissist to "suddenly" act this way (Miller, n.d.). Since the HSP can easily sense when something is wrong, they mistakenly believe they must be responsible for fixing the problem. A narcissist jumps on this trait and will use it to their advantage (Marlow-MaCoy, 2018).

This relationship phase will put the HSP into a never-ending downward-spiralling loop. They'll reach out, trying to help the narcissist and find out what's wrong. The narcissist will likely play the victim, preying on the HSP's compassionate side. It will draw the HSP in even further. After the HSP has given all their energy, attention and affirmation to the narcissist, the narcissist will show a little breadcrumb of love. This will remind the HSP of the early connected stages of the relationship and ease the current tension to make the HSP happy again. After that, it's right back to the new norm of being cold and distant for the narcissist.

Gathering tiny breadcrumbs of love, the HSP continues starving in the relationship, tolerating abusive and insulting treatment. Each time, for a moment, they see a glimpse of what the relationship used to be and believe that if they keep trying, they can bring back the connection and affection they used to experience with the narcissist. That crusty moment makes them feel what they're doing is working, even if it's just for a little while. Throughout this stage and beyond, the narcissist will begin to diminish the value of the HSP. They will engage in various forms of emotional abuse, especially gaslighting. *Gaslighting* is when someone denies your reality and imposes their perspective on you. "You're being too sensitive." Gaslighting refuses to validate your feelings and affirm you in your experiences. Instead, the gaslighter says you are selfish in the situation or your behaviour is dramatic and crazy. This is an especially dangerous manipulation tool. It's one of the narcissist's favourite ways to get their partners (especially HSPs) to start disconnecting with themselves, ignoring their instincts, losing trust in themselves, and turning to the narcissist as the "fount of all knowledge" and control.

Even though the HSP is experiencing abuse, the narcissist will attempt to make them believe it's their weakness or sensitivity, making them feel off in the relationship. With surface-level considerations, the narcissist will convince the HSP that they are treated very well in the relationship. (Miller, n.d.)

The Aftermath

This cycle continues, and over time, it begins to break the HSP down. They become disconnected from themselves, distrusting their intuition and doubting their reality, common symptoms of gaslighting and emotional abuse.

As the victim of narcissistic abuse, you will believe the other person (the gaslighter) is in the right. So, you choose them as the standard of truth and ignore your different gut feelings about the relationship. The reasons people stay in abusive relationships are varied, but in this case, the narcissist has built their trap effectively. They have used the loop to their advantage, repeatedly pushing away and drawing in their prey. And suppose the HSP has a past of trauma or abuse. In that case, this familiarity can be especially hard for them to recognize and break. For some, this cycle has been a part of their life for so long that they might not know how to relate any other way.

But another aspect of HSPs which makes them particularly vulnerable to this kind of abuse is that they believe they can achieve something if they work hard enough. Usually, they tend to be hard-working and conscientious people. They are also unique in that they can see things others may not. As I mentioned before, that may make them feel almost obligated to do something about whatever they see since they have the "gift" of being able to see it.

On top of that, the HSP in a narcissistic relationship will believe that if they just keep working harder, acting more compassionately, and being more loving, they will eventually be able to return to that dreamy love-bombing stage. Sadly though, the narcissist knows this and will continue to take just as much as the HSP struggles to give. They will even demand more and the cycle will not end until the relationship ends.

In addition to the mental and emotional toll this kind of relationship will take on the HSP, there will also often be physical responses. The HSP might suffer from stomach troubles, fatigue, inability to sleep, racing heartbeat, headaches, and more. Unfortunately, these negative feelings might make the HSP do anything possible to avoid them. They will keep trying hard to make the narcissist happy so they can finally relax. But the HSP will find themselves constantly needing to walk on eggshells, and any momentary peace is soon interrupted.

Conclusion

The line between the narcissist and the highly sensitive person is sure to become blurry, codependency will abound, and all the unique and beautiful attributes of the HSP will at some point be put on an altar as a sacrifice to appease the insatiable appetite of the narcissist. By the end of one of these relationships, the HSP will feel completely exhausted and drained, their very soul crushed from their time, energy and resources invested into the narcissist.

Typically, a relationship between a narcissist and a highly sensitive person will end in one of two ways. The narcissist will abruptly discard the HSP, dropping all contact and communication when they find a more appealing source for the praise and admiration needed to fuel their life. Or, the highly sensitive person will begin to recognize the toxicity of the relationship and the immense damage it has done, and they will intentionally make a plan to leave. Whether you made a choice or not, the removal of oneself from the suffocating grip of a narcissist is a messy and complicated endeavour which will require a period of recovery.

There are plenty of books out there about narcissists and the havoc they wreak in relationships with any person. The negativity and hopelessness of such relationships are not the focus of this book. Even if HSPs are common prey to narcissistic abuse, you don't have to remain a victim! By learning about your nature and developing healing habits, you can nurture and protect yourself so you will never again fall into the trap of a narcissist.

Our journey together will focus mainly on what happens after you've gotten out of your relationship with the narcissist. I want to discuss the beautiful healing work you can do to find freedom, simplicity and sanctuary in your life. There is always the potential of finding another friend, mentor or partner who loves and supports you and will not seek to manipulate and control you to win your attention and affection.

Worth and value are inherent in every individual, and every person (including you!) is sacred, deserving of love and the highest respect. As HSPs, we are exceptionally skilled at loving and caring for others, but if we are to be truly healthy and prosperous in our own lives and relationships, we must learn to say "yes" to ourselves, "yes" to our needs, and "yes" to our desires. This may not come naturally, but by recognizing the weight of our own significance, we can recover from the harm of past abusive relationships and build a new and secure future. To do this, we must consider our sensitive natures and, through intentional practice, cultivate safe and sacred spaces for ourselves.

If you suspect you are entangled in the grasp of a narcissist, but you're not entirely sure, you can ask yourself these questions to evaluate your situation. Evaluating a relationship, even a good one, is always healthy since it promotes self-reflection and connection to yourself. This fosters confidence and belief in your capacity to make the right decisions for your life (something the narcissist does not want you to do)!

Start here by honestly asking yourself:

- How do I feel overall about my relationship? (When I think about it, what is the general feeling? Stress, anxiety, happiness, support?)

- Do I have any recent physical ailments that seem unexplained? Stress-related ailments like stomach trouble or migraines?

- When I think of my partner (or friend or relative), what comes to mind?

- Do I often find myself feeling guilty?

- Do our arguments often end with me feeling like I'm in the wrong or like the argument has been twisted out of my control?

- How do I feel when my partner/friend/relative is at home? How do I feel when they are away?

- How does my relationship compare to other relationships I see?

Take some time for yourself as you take your first steps toward your recovery. From personal experience, I know how difficult it can be to remember you have the strength and power to make your own decisions (and good ones too). It can seem like a huge step to start thinking about breaking off such a domineering relationship, but taking time on your own to meditate on your thoughts and feelings will help you reconnect with yourself and harness the strength lying dormant inside. It's time to break free from the destructive bond between you and the narcissist in your life.

Summary

This chapter focused on the destructive bond between HSPs and narcissists. I also discussed the following:

- the reason why HSPs can be particularly vulnerable to narcissistic abuse
- how narcissists tend to behave in relationships
- how the vicious downward-spiralling loop begins
- how HSPs can begin to think about leaving and starting their recovery.

In chapter three, I want to discuss the topic of how highly sensitive people and their personality relates to the *Myers-Briggs* personality type system. Remember, the more you know about yourself, the better you can build boundaries, create a better life, and have healthier relationships.

Understand and Celebrate Your Personality

Perhaps because we are innately and naturally self-interested, we often find the study of personality types fascinating. We always want to know which category we fit or what label we might fall under. Likely, you've taken at least one personality test in your time to figure out those answers. Life can be somewhat chaotic and unplanned, and uncontrollable. But learning about ourselves and others and what makes us tick can help give us just a little feeling of control.

And as HSPs, that desire for a little more control and understanding can be even stronger. As HSPs, we naturally create a rich inner world for ourselves, but when we get into abusive relationships, the vibrancy of our lives is steadily diminished. Once free of abuse, you can build yourself up again by reconnecting to the sacred and unique space inside yourself. This process is more straightforward with the help of personality diagnosing tools.

Suppose you're unaware of your high sensitivity. In that case, you can easily feel like a mutant weirdo compared to everyone else around you. Things feel overwhelming to you that might be very normal and relaxing to another person. You can't understand it! It's frustrating; sometimes, you just wish you were "normal." I get it. I've been there. But with more understanding about your personality type, you can leave behind the idea that you're a freak and start to look at yourself in a new, fresh, and positive light.

The History of Myers-Briggs

If you've taken a personality test before or multiple, likely you've taken at least one that was a *Myers-Briggs* personality type test. If not, you've at least likely heard of it and also heard of the strange collection of letters that goes with it: ENFJ, INFP, etc.

Isabel Myers and Katherine Briggs, a mother and daughter psychological team, created the Myers-Briggs personality types and tests because they were fascinated by Carl Jung's work on personality types. Jung looked at how people preferred to interact with the world and divided them into categories such as extroversion and introversion. But these two ladies took his work on personality types a step further (Cherry, 2021a).

During *World War II*, they began to develop an assessment that would be able to sort people into 16 personality types. It could help people discover their differences, strengths, and preferences. Their original goal was to assist people in finding an occupation that would best suit them and their personality type. These women created a test with questions that would help divide people into the proper categories. The test has been expanded and developed since the 1940s, but it began then (Cherry, 2021a).

The Types

Just to give you a general idea of how it works, the test assessment is divided into four scales:

1. Extroversion (E) - Introversion (I): outward-turning vs. inward-turning

2. Sensing (S) - iNtuition (N): focused on facts and reality vs. more creative/imaginative

3. Thinking (T) - Feeling (F): how people make decisions (brain or gut)

4. Judging (J) - Perceiving (P): more rigid vs. more flexible on decisions

After a person takes the test, they receive four letters which denote their behavioural preferences. There are 16 preferences:

ISTJ, ISTP, ISFJ, ISFP

INFJ, INFP, INTJ, INTP

ESTP, ESTJ, ESFP, ESFJ

ENFP, ENFJ, ENTP, ENTJ

Even though some may bristle at getting a label or being "put into a box," learning at least a little about your personality type can benefit your personal and work life. Note, there isn't one type which is superior to the others. All styles are equal, and they each have value in the world.

The HSP and Myers-Briggs Connection

Interestingly, being highly sensitive is a prevalent trait in certain *Myers-Briggs* personality types, especially INFJs and INFPs. Those with preferences for Introversion, iNtuition and Feeling have a particular connection to the highly sensitive attribute. For fun, someone performed an informal "study" in one of their HSP social media groups to see how far that connection between being highly sensitive and having a particular *Myers-Briggs* personality type went.

The study consisted of an informal Facebook poll in an HSP Facebook group, asking people for their *Myers-Briggs* personality type. The host read the results, assuming that everyone in the group was indeed an HSP and that they knew their actual *Myers-Briggs* type. The host was able to gather around 500 responses! Take a look at the results here, which were posted on the site INF Club (2019):

INFJ	216
INFP	152
ENFP	34
ISFJ	23
INTJ	15
ENFJ	10
ISFP	6
INTP	4
ISTJ	3
ENTJ	1
ESTJ	1
ESFJ	1
ISTP	1
ENTP	1
ESFP	0
ESTP	0
total = 468	

Wow! About 80 percent of the HSPs were either INFJ or INFP. And more of the HSPs are INFJ. This is surprising when you consider that INFJs are the rarest personality type, occurring in only 1-2 percent of the population. Of course, this is not a perfect study, but it's an interesting connection. Take another look at the scales in the personality test. You'll see INFJ is Introverted iNtuitive Feeling Judging, and INFP is Introverted iNtuitive Feeling Perceiving. If you haven't taken a Myers-Briggs test before, take one, and see where you fit in! As for me, I am falling right into the norm: both highly sensitive and an INFJ.

Are All HSPs INFJs?

So, are all HSPs INFJs? Although this study isn't foolproof, it demonstrates that this is not the case. Not all HSPs are INFJs, but it's more likely that all INFJs are also HSPs. Let's take a look at a deeper description of an INFJ personality type, and you can see the significant similarities. INFJs:

- are gentle, caring, kind, compassionate people
- are clued into other people's emotions/feelings
- gravitate towards caring jobs
- dislike conflict/violence and will try to avoid it
- are sensitive to stress and will receive physical effects from it

- prefer deep, meaningful connections with people as opposed to just small talk
- like that one-on-one time as opposed to larger group activities
- have an internal life and focus
- want to continuously pursue personal growth and development (Ward, 2017).

You can certainly see the similarities! But while an INFJ will usually turn out to also be an HSP, it doesn't always follow that an HSP has to be an INFJ.

Jung's 8 Cognitive Functions

This chapter is not just for INFJs. In addition to the four scales of preference described above, you can also understand the 16 types through the lens of Jung's original work to distinguish eight cognitive functions. These functions relate to how we take in information, process it and use it to make decisions. Each of the 16 types has a first (dominant), second (auxiliary), third (tertiary) and fourth (inferior) preference as it relates to cognitive function. This is a bit technical but stay with me. The dominant and auxiliary functions are your strongest preferences or strengths, and the tertiary and inferior functions are those with which you struggle. (Sidenote: although there are eight cognitive functions, you are likely only consciously accessing 4 of them. The other 4 are subconscious functions known as "shadow functions." However, if you intentionally do the inner work, you may be able to integrate all eight functions and, by doing so, experience an extremely high level of emotional and interpersonal wellness.)

When you take a *Myers-Briggs Type Indicator*™ (MBTI) test, you might have trouble answering the assessment questions, or you might get a result that is somewhat well-fitting but not completely. For example, it wasn't until I understood the eight cognitive functions that I could correctly type myself as an INFJ. I had previously mistaken myself for being an INTJ and then an INFP.

By now, you are probably getting curious about your personality type. Here is a brief description of each cognitive function. You will have either the introverted or the extroverted expression of each N, F, S, and T. Which two cognitive functions do you most lean toward?

Introverted iNtuition (Ni) – If you've noticed and internalized patterns or appreciated symbolism or metaphor, you may be uniquely skilled with Introverted iNtuition. Others see those with Ni as mystical or spiritual people and are often amazed at how they just "know" things. Those with this rare trait are abstract thinkers and find it nearly impossible to explain the processes happening in their minds to put all the information together so they can understand it holistically. Led by "gut feeling," those with Ni are incredibly creative and insightful individuals.

- Ni Dominant types: INTJs, INFJs; Auxiliary types: ENFJs, ENTJs

Extroverted iNtuition (Ne) – Those with strengths in Extroverted iNtuition perceive patterns and abstractions in the external world, such as with people or events. They love new challenges and experiences, which provide fuel for thinking up theories, possibilities and potentials. They are very curious and will explore a new idea as far as it can go, always asking, "what if...?"

- Ne Dominant types: ENTPs, ENFPs; Auxiliary types: INFPs, INTPs

Introverted Feeling (Fi) – A person with solid Introverted Feeling reflects on the full spectrum of their emotions and is whole-heartedly committed to living authentically in alignment with their personal values. This often means they reject the expectations put on them by others and live with fierce individuality. They are most at home in non-judgmental spaces where they feel accepted for who they are. Perhaps this is why they are often drawn to children, animals and nature.

- Fi Dominant types: INFPs, ISFPs; Auxiliary types: ENFPs, ESFPs

Extroverted Feeling (Fe) – Extroverted Feeling means that you are more concerned with the feelings of those around you than your own. Those strong in Fe value community and emotional connection with those around them. In social settings, they strive to create consensus and morale. They may choose caring careers like social work and possess high emotional intelligence, which is why their friends value them highly for support.

- Fe Dominant types: ENFJs, ESFJs; Auxiliary types: INFJs, ISFJs

Introverted Sensing (Si) – This function is all about recalling and appreciating experiences associated with the physical senses. Those with prominent Introverted Sensing will internalize their experiences and then draw on those memories to make decisions, prop up their beliefs or decide how to behave in a similar situation. They love and uphold tradition and what is familiar.

- Si Dominant types: ISTJs, ISFJs; Auxiliary types: ESTJs, ESFJs

Extroverted Sensing (Se) – Those with high Se are constantly watching for, taking in and responding to information about the world around them through their senses. They have a strong awareness of the physical sensations in their bodies and live very much in the present moment. This is the sort of person you want to have around when an emergency happens because they will be quick to respond and know what to do.

- Se Dominant types: ESTPs, ESFPs; Auxiliary types: ISTPs, ISFPs

Introverted Thinking (Ti) – Introverted Thinkers are preoccupied with internalizing data and are often perceived by others as "living in their heads." They appreciate logic and reason and seek to analyze and understand the essence of a thing, boiling the information down to the lowest common denominator. Those with this strength are excellent problem solvers, adapting and flexible with their ideas.

- Ti Dominant types: INTPs, ISTPs; Auxiliary types: ENTPs, ESTPs

Extroverted Thinking (Te) – Those strong in Extroverted Thinking will put aside their feelings to make decisions based solely on logic and facts. They like to examine the evidence of a matter and make evaluations by weighing out the pros and cons or considering the cause and effect.

Extroverted Thinkers are very goal-oriented and make good organizational leaders because they care about categorizing their environments and creating structures to maximize effectiveness.

- Te Dominant types: ENTJs, ESTJs; Auxiliary types: INTJs, ISTJs

Cognitive Functions Related to HSPs

Of course, there are always anomalies, but my personal hypothesis is that the combination of first (dominant) and second (auxiliary) preferences for the cognitive functions of both Introverted iNtuition (Ni) and Extraverted Feeling (Fe) makes for a very very high chance of also being an HSP. But having the reverse combination, Extroverted iNtuition (Ne) and Introverted Feeling (Fi) follows closely behind. Simply scoring high on the scale in only one of the first four cognitive functions I listed (Ni, Ne, Fi, Fe), in either the dominant or auxiliary preference position, will be enough to indicate you as an HSP, and all the more if it's Ni or Fe.

Conclusion

My advice is this: if you haven't taken a *Myers-Briggs* personality test, jump online and do so! Once you take the test, you'll get your result with a more detailed explanation of your personality type. Now that you know about your highly sensitive personality, taking this test can help flesh out your personality further and give you even greater insight into the wonderful world of you.

My goal is for you to enjoy building up your inner life again. To help you celebrate your beautiful, unique personhood in the world. As individuals, we should all be honoured for our gifts and who we are as people. And as HSPs, we have so much to offer, and if you know your strengths, you can use them to your advantage.

As I keep saying, the more you know about yourself, the better you can navigate the world, the better you will be able to make good decisions for yourself! And it will help you avoid situations that could have a significant adverse effect on your life, such as getting involved with a narcissist. So get to know yourself, and you can get to know a more fruitful path for your life.

Summary

This chapter discussed the connection between the *Myers-Briggs* personality test and the HSP. It also covered:

- the history of *Myers-Briggs* and its purpose
- the type results typical to HSPs
- descriptions of Jung's eight cognitive functions to help you identify your type

The next section of this book is about the healing habits you can implement in your life to recover from abuse. Together we will focus on building a new foundation for the construction of your new life after getting out of narcissistic abuse. Your healing will prepare you for a brighter future. On to the habits!

Part Two: Cultivate Healing Habits

The Mindset for Starting Over

Let's return to our relatable story from the introduction. Tabitha spent years in a marriage with her narcissist husband, Derrick. After everything went down, they divorced and finally went their separate ways. Tabitha, feeling things as keenly as she did due to her high sensitivity, felt broken and used up. She had no idea where to go from there. She'd finally had the courage to make a significant life decision and escape the abuse. Still, she was left alone, trying to pick up the pieces of her former self again.

I've been in that place before. Have you? Even if a breakup is a positive choice for you and your life, it's very common to feel a little bit empty afterwards. You had a relationship, marriage, or even a deep friendship with someone, and now it's just over. Sometimes, you can start to regret leaving or at least second-guess the breakup.

Don't give in to these feelings. Even if they are normal, just give yourself a little time to get through the hard part of the breakup, and you will begin to see things in a better light. If you were in a relationship with a narcissist, then separation is the best and only option. There is no hope for change, and it will only get worse. Remember: you deserve a relationship and a partner that gives you support and love, one that doesn't make you feel worthless or crazy.

As discussed in the last chapter, there are two modes of living: introverted and extroverted. Our introverted mode is how we conduct ourselves in the sacred space of our mind. It is the thoughts and mindsets we have which create our beliefs and values. These, in turn, influence the decisions we make and the actions we take on a daily basis. Our extroverted mode is how we interact with the world outside ourselves; the environments of home, work and leisure and the many relationships in which we participate. When we are healthy in the introverted space, self-mastered and confident of our worth and value, we are much better equipped to create and maintain the life we want to live in the various contexts outside ourselves.

THE MINDSET FOR STARTING OVER 57

You need healing habits in your toolbox as you begin your recovery journey. It helped me immensely to study, contemplate, and work hard to heal from my abusive marriage, and I want to help you do the same. The first habits, which are mainly introverted, will help you refocus your extroverted life and goals on what is truly important: helping and loving yourself. They will help you re-establish your sacred inner space and understand the unique self you've been missing in your life for so long. We'll focus first on building inward habits of gratitude, positive affirmation, and meaning. Then we will shift our focus outward through mindfulness and turn our focus to the extroverted habits of authenticity, self-care, and connection.

It's All About the Mindset

Okay, I know the word "mindset" is a little overused. People often make it so easy, saying, "Just have a good mindset, and everything's going to be okay!" But then, they provide no other information, and you're left feeling angry and resentful. Of course, no one wants to hear that kind of thing right when they're in the middle of heartbreak and grief. But I'm going to approach this a little differently with specificity. I agree that a proper mindset is essential, but there is much more to it.

According to Carol Dweck, a Stanford psychologist, having the right mindset impacts your success or failure in whatever you're trying to do. Since you're now free of your abusive relationship, it's time to tend to the soil of your mindset so that the new habits we are planting together can get established, grow and produce a harvest so you can enjoy the fruit of all your inner work.

A mindset is your belief system about something, affecting how you think, feel, and act in various situations. Have you ever heard someone say something to you like, "Oh, you're just not going into it with the right mindset"? These beliefs make up who you are and how you interact with the world. There are two different mindsets: fixed and growth. When your thoughts, ideas and opinions are firmly set in place, you are unwilling to consider new possibilities or change how you think about something, you have a fixed mindset. Focusing on growth, progress, and change will be tough with this mindset. It's like a garden full of rocks and sandy soil—there's no room for new plants, and the environment is too harsh for anything but weeds to grow. This mindset means you believe your abilities and talents are stuck in one place, and that's just it. A fixed mindset might sound like, "Either I'm good at this, or I'm not," or "If I have to work hard at something, that means I'm not good at it."

This kind of mindset gets you nowhere. After a breakup or any heartbreaking situation, it can be so easy to remain in this mindset because you're so used to it. Dark thoughts cross your mind.

"No one loves me because I'm hard to love."

"I can't seem to hold onto anybody."

"I don't know how to be in a relationship."

"I guess I'll be alone for the rest of my life."

"He (the narcissistic abuser) was right about me. I'm impossible to be with."

Those thoughts will keep you in the same place after you remove yourself from the abusive relationship. Unfortunately, this mindset has no room or space to grow and move forward. And as an HSP, these feelings can be especially powerful and daunting, keeping you firmly in one place (much to the satisfaction of your former abuser!).

A growth mindset is entirely different. Sure, you still have your beliefs, but there is an important distinction. A growth mindset focuses on expansion and change, leaving the door open to healing and progress. It's like a garden with freshly tilled soil, ready to receive seeds of change, constantly growing and producing healthy and nourishing thoughts. For example, in a fixed mindset, you might think, "I'm just not good at that," but in a growth mindset, that same thought would sound more like, "I can learn to do anything I put my mind to."

With this kind of mindset, you might look at your former abusive relationship more like this:

"It wasn't my fault that he/she acted that way."

"There are other people out there that are compatible with me."

"I have a bright future in which good things will happen."

Some people may think this kind of mindset means you're ignoring truth and reality. A growth mindset can be challenging because it may feel like a pipe dream. After you get out of a long-term relationship, it's stretching to think there could be a future with somebody else. Everything looks dark and daunting in front of you.

However, this mindset will become more familiar to navigate the more you work with it. And at the same time, it gives you the space you need to heal from the abuse you've experienced. So, even if you may not feel it, a growth mindset will open you to beautiful possibilities and help you move forward to embrace your full potential and a prosperous future.

Why Do We Have Our Mindsets?

There's no one correct answer to this question, but our mindsets are a product of how we've grown up and the circumstances to which we were exposed. Our thought formation has a lot to do with what our parents and teachers did and how they spoke to us about our achievements. Dweck studied the kind of praise children receive and how it affects their mindset. For example, praising a certain way, like labelling, puts people in a box. Suppose a child proudly wears the label "smart." In that case, she can believe she has no ability in a specific area if she does not receive the "smart" title. This kind of labelling/praise can lead people to believe they either have the skill or they don't (a fixed mindset idea).

But suppose parents/teachers praise the process instead. They emphasize hard work, organization skills or preparation instead of focusing only on the result. This way of relating goes a long way to developing a growth mindset for the child. Here's an example: "I'm impressed with how well you studied and prepared for your exam. You organized your notes, and you spent time each day reviewing. Great job!"

Many of us were praised with labels, making us settle and fix ideas about ourselves in our belief system; we either have the skill or we don't. We are either intelligent or stupid. People like us, or they don't. We will have success in relationships, or we won't. Fixed mindsets are common; for HSPs, we latch onto things tighter than others. Praise, especially in the form of labels, affects us deeply. When we receive any form of recognition, we take it to heart.

This kind of mindset can be detrimental to us. "Popular," "intelligent," "artsy," "weird," and "athletic" we grew up being organized into boxes and categories and told to stay there. But people don't always behave in the boxed way we expect. Life doesn't behave in an organized fashion either, and often, we find we are more complex than our parents and teachers ever thought. With all its intricate layers, life is not about conforming to our particular labels. You're an adult now. After years of living in a fixed mindset, I would challenge you to work on developing a growth mindset.

Instead of looking at obstacles as final or as roadblocks, you can begin to look at them as opportunities. We can focus on what happened (getting out of an abusive relationship, yay!) and use those positive aspects as fuel to move forward.

THE MINDSET FOR STARTING OVER

What's Your Mindset? Do You Need a Change?

Part of the healing journey is to take time with yourself to reflect and meditate. You can evaluate which mindset you have with contemplation.

Take a look at these statements and their explanations (Cherry, 2021b), and evaluate how you feel about them to discover whether your mindset is fixed or growth-oriented:

1. The intelligence you're born with can't be changed.

2. You can't improve your basic abilities or personality.

3. People are capable of changing their temperaments and identity.

4. You can always learn new things and improve your knowledge and intelligence.

5. People either have particular talents or they don't. You can't just pick up a skill in music, writing, art, or sports.

6. Studying, working hard, and practicing are all ways to gain new talents and abilities.

You probably have a fixed mindset if you agree heartily with numbers 1, 2, and 5. But if you agree greatly with numbers 3, 4, and 6, you have a growth mindset!

But if you have a fixed mindset, how can you change it? It'll take work, no doubt, but it is possible. Start by focusing on the journey. Remember praising the process? By reading and applying the strategies in this book, you are well on your way to a better future. It takes courage to change your reality. I applaud you for bravely considering how you can build a strong foundation for the future. Here I am, right now, praising you on your process instead of focusing on the end goal (finding complete healing from your abusive relationship). Considering your recovery journey, take one step at a time, and you will heal bit by bit from the abuse you've gone through. I want you to stop worrying about getting to a particular end destination or even comparing yourself to others' similar journeys. My healing journey is different from yours, and yours will be different from mine. There is no exact formula or timeline. Enjoy the process. You are already well on your way!

Next, start adding the word "yet" to the sentences you say to yourself. Instead of, "I don't know how to do that" or "I am not over the relationship," try adding "yet" to the end of those sentences. Sure, you're in one place where things look dark, but the "yet" implies a bright future; there is hope for change and development.

Also, try adjusting how you speak and think to yourself and how you see the world to be more positive. I know this takes work because staying where you are is comfortable. It feels good (because it's easy and familiar!) to sit and say dark, hopeless statements such as, "I'll never be good enough." Still, in the end, those kinds of comments don't get you anywhere. They keep you in that negative space, and eventually, whatever depressing thing you're thinking and saying to yourself will prove itself true. Change your inner dialogue to more positive statements, such as, "I haven't felt good enough for a long time, but the truth is, I am good enough."

Lastly, and this is a big one, start taking on challenges or doing things that frighten you. As HSPs, when we make mistakes, the resulting negative feelings are so strong compared to non-HSPs. These feelings can make you want to shy away from difficult or new things and situations. Still, again, this will only prevent you from growing and keep you in that fixed mindset. And that won't help you as you're trying to heal from the pain of your relationship.

Around the time I began seriously considering the life-altering change of leaving my abusive partner, I decided to do a thing that scared me. I stumbled upon some online videos of a woman who used beautiful silk flags to dance to Christian worship music in church settings and alone in nature. This beautiful and whole-hearted expression so compelled me that I purchased my own set of flowing white silk flags. I practiced dancing alone in my living room when no one was around but what I actually wanted to do was dance during worship time at church. I was terrified that people would readily see that I was clumsy, lacked grace, and had no formal dance experience or training. I wondered if they would judge me for such an exuberant expression, but it was a sincere desire in my heart. So I began to bring my flags with me to church. A few weeks passed with them sitting limply on the pew before I threw my fears to the wind and stepped out into the aisle. But, I did it; I danced in public at church, not for people's attention, but as an expression of love for my God. It was one of the most authentic moments of my life. Afterwards, many people affirmed my actions and now flagging, as it is sometimes referred to, is a regular part of my worship expression.

I tell you that story because I honestly believe that stepping out and doing something I was afraid to do in that smaller context gave me the courage, and fostered the mindset shift I needed, to do the next harder and scarier thing in my life. On a fateful day a few months later, when my then-husband left the house for the afternoon, I packed my children and as many necessities as I could into the back of the SUV, and I drove away from my abusive marriage relationship forever.

Summary

Your introverted world is likely in shambles after a relationship with a narcissist. You will need a growth mindset to reverse the damage and grow to recover. In this chapter, we looked at the following:

- What mindset is, and how it affects us

- Why you have your mindset

- The critical differences between a fixed and a growth mindset

- How you can posture your mindset to be a growth mindset.

In the next chapter, we will look at the introverted habits of gratitude, positive affirmation, and meaning.

Introverted Healing Habits

HOW WE CONDUCT OURSELVES internally will determine the quality of our external living and being. Though they can be expressed in an extroverted way, the perspectives we form, the messages we tell ourselves, and the intentions around how we want to show up in the world are all processes happening beneath the surface. That's why, in this chapter, we will examine the introverted healing habits of gratitude, positive affirmation, and living a meaningful life by identifying our core values.

Let's Start Here

After you've been through a difficult situation, whatever it may be, the last thing you want is to hear people say, "focus on being positive/happy/grateful"!

Of course, that is part of your healing, but let's start at the beginning before we delve into the habit of gratitude.

You are hurt. You're heartbroken and grieving after you broke off your relationship. Even if it was a situation in which you suffered abuse, there is still grief, and that's okay. One of the best things I did at the start of my healing journey was to acknowledge that I was grieving. People may have wanted me to be happy instantly because I was finally away from the abuse. I was free from the narcissistic reach of my husband, and I was out in the world again, independent and free. But, while my freedom was a fantastic relief, I was heartbroken. I had double grief. First, I had to acknowledge honestly to myself that the person I thought I married never actually existed but was, in fact, a delusion in my mind, a carefully crafted and manipulated image presented skillfully to me by my narcissistic partner. Second, I had to grieve my ex-husband's true nature, that he never truly loved *me* but only valued how I served *his* needs and what I could do for *him*. And also, the familiar life we shared, though difficult, was now over and gone.

Loss is a fitting way to describe it because when you cut out a narcissist from your life, it is like a significant part of you has died. It has passed away, and now you've got to start a whole new life without it. So again, it was a good thing my relationship was "dead," but at the same time, it was a massive part of my life, and I felt a loss deep down inside.

Acknowledge and accept whatever feelings and thoughts head your way during this time. As an HSP, you will experience grief and loss very deeply. Let it be. Do not care what others say about how you should feel or how quickly you should get over something. That's reminiscent of the narcissistic abuse you've gone through already: someone telling you what you're experiencing isn't true. So, acknowledge your hurt and pain; let it pass through you, and then you will be ready to start healing habits of recovery, starting with gratitude.

The Habit of Gratitude: Recognize Beauty and Goodness Even Amid Grief and Pain

One of the best habits you can implement in your life is the habit of gratitude. It's a beneficial habit for anyone, not just HSPs or those recovering from abuse. Recognizing the good around you can be a life preserver in a sea of grief and pain. It's effortless to dwell on the negative, especially after we're hurt. However, if we are to progress, grow, and move on after our painful experiences and abuse, we need to realize that there are good things in life and the world around us. Even right now, amid your great unhappiness, there is something good to see and be grateful for.

Gratitude is a state of being. We would classify it as a positive emotion, acknowledging the good and happy things in our lives. This recognition leads us to thankfulness. It's a process, though, and it takes time, just like any other good thing.

The steps from the site *Narcissistic Abuse Support* (n.d.) are as follows:

1. Recognize the good things. Think specifically about what is good for you, not just anyone in general.

2. Let yourself feel positive about these good things. That can be tricky! But it's about allowing ourselves to feel a good and happy feeling in relation to these positive things in our day-to-day life.

The point is to start changing and shifting our perspective. Right now, all you might be able to see is the darkness and sadness, but gratitude can help pull your gaze away from the gloom and into the light. This habit will help you move beyond the first stage of grief and into the healing world of a new life. Essentially, you are asking yourself daily, "What is good?"

In the immediate aftermath of my decision to leave my abusive partner, I found myself needing to wake up at 5 am to make lunches for myself and my children and to get us all up, dressed, breakfasted, and into the car to make the hour-long commute to daycare and work. We had moved into my parents' 70s-style basement, which included a bathroom with a stall shower and exposed copper pipes overhead. The cold water pipe would always accumulate ice-cold condensation, and while I was sudsing up, I would be startled rudely by the intrusion of the frigid drips. But even in this less-than-ideal context, I shifted my mind into gratitude gear. I would consider the alternative, the ugly situation I had left behind, and thanksgiving would flood my thoughts. *I am grateful to be able to live here, where I am respected and valued. I am so thankful for a job to go to and the provision of daycare for my children. Here, I am free from control and criticism; here, I can rest and make a plan for a better future.* In addition, the gas price fell drastically at that time because of certain world events, so even though I was commuting further than ever for work, the gas was dirt cheap. I was emotionally and physically exhausted but continually reminding myself of what was good helped to keep me moving through this most challenging phase of turning my life around.

After abuse, there can be much fear. This fear leads to anxiety which may keep you from enjoying life and bringing yourself happiness. But studies have shown that implementing positive practices such as gratitude can help reduce this fear or, rather, the reaction to the fear, such as withdrawal. So, let's put creating a habit of gratitude into your toolbox!

There are many ways to go about it, and it's up to you. Many find gratitude journaling can be a great way to see an actual list of what you're grateful for and why. But journaling isn't for everyone. A simple process of daily meditation, meditating on what you're thankful for, can be just as effective. Perhaps you could even think of something you're grateful for and be sure to say it at least once a day to someone or just to yourself. Maybe you use each negative thought that comes into your mind as a trigger and cue to look for and consider something positive for which you can be thankful. These methods help promote this habit. Be intentional and choose what works for your personality and your life right now. Remember, it takes time! Some studies on this practice state that it takes about eight months for its effects to be truly felt. (Moore, n.d.).

The Habit of Positive Affirmation: Verbal Declarations to Pave a New Path

Remember when we talked about having a fixed mindset? We may have many beliefs that are difficult to eliminate because they are deeply embedded within us. It is as if we have carved thinking pathways into our brains, and because those pathways are so often trodden, they are the paths of least resistance. An abusive relationship with a narcissist will gouge deep, dark trails in our thinking.

Often, as the abuse is prolonged or when we finally cut it off, we find we barely know or understand ourselves anymore. There is no self-love or self-confidence, and it's almost like you've got to start from the beginning, building yourself back up to what you had before you met your abuser. This is where positive affirmations come in. I know it might sound strange or ridiculous if you've never engaged in using affirmations before, but they can work wonders.

Because our adverse thought pathways have been so deeply etched into our minds, made worse by a relationship with a narcissist, we need to start changing the voice inside our heads. I know the voice within is probably shouting that you're not good enough. It lies and says your identity is what the narcissist abuser said, or it condemns you as unworthy of a healthy and fulfilling relationship. Whatever negative lines are repeating in your mind, it's time to overwrite the message so you can take back control of your life. Standing up for yourself and talking back to that dark voice with positive affirmations is like venturing off the worn path wielding a machete, cutting down the thick overgrown branches in front of your face as you bushwack a new and better way forward. Go ahead and get violent with old thought patterns.

These affirmations can be very simple, such as, "I have value," or a little more complex and specific, such as Tabitha saying, "I don't need Derrick to tell me who I am."

These affirmations carve new and brighter pathways of thought that bring about positivity and progress, turning your gaze from the darkness to the light! They will bring you back to your reality, which had been stolen from you by the narcissistic abuser. Your whole inner world needs to be recreated, and this is simply done when you use your voice to speak kind words of truth to yourself. Words are powerful and creative by nature. Just think about all the words that come together to make this sentence. All the sentences in this chapter make a central idea and all the ideas on these pages you are holding make a book. But boil it all down, and you get words. Words are powerful.

Here it is good to note that victims who leave abusive relationships will often experience setbacks by going back to their narcissist after a period of separation. I, myself, made this mistake, believing the beautiful words of the narc as he wielded them to paint the picture I most longed to see. The narcissist does not readily want to let someone out of their control, so, with their words, they will try to lure you back. Remember, words are powerful. They will craft their words precisely, tailoring them to what you want to hear. But don't fall for the manipulation. The narc has no intention of *doing* what he says or matching his *actions* to the words. He simply does not want to lose the benefits your relationship provided, nor does he want to lose control. Be prepared for this. Daily speaking positive affirmations about you, your worth, and your ability can help you withstand whatever schemes the narcissist might attempt to bring you back under his control.

After you end a relationship with this kind of abuser, it's best to do so by going "no contact," if possible. That's the safest way because the narcissist speaks the precise words you want to hear to get you to come back. That's why you need to arm yourself and fight back with your *own* words to yourself. They've spent the last however long in your relationship breaking you down, but you can bring yourself back up!

An exercise I found very beneficial was to think about lies I told myself or believed strongly. I wrote them out and then replaced each lie with an affirming statement to myself. I wrote these in a little notebook and reviewed them daily until it felt more natural to believe them. These are specific to me and incorporate my faith, but they may also help you:

"I choose to accept my sacred and God-given identity."

"I am significant."

"God has good things in store for me."

"I am creatively expressive."

"I am worth the extra effort."

"God cares for and treasures my feelings."

"I choose to be present and seen."

"I commit to embracing my authentic self so I can receive love and acceptance from true friends."

I found saying affirmations so transformative to myself that I started using them with my children. Whenever my kids came to me in tears after getting hurt, I asked them to repeat after me. We would say, "I am strong. I am brave. I am okay." Then they would jump up and start playing again. If one of my children said something mean or rude to the other, I would have them correct their hurtful words with kind ones. I posted affirming sticky notes above their beds to be reviewed nightly at bedtime, and my 5-year-old told me he would sleep so much better with them there. It's never too early or too late to start a positive conversation with yourself!

These are something you can say to yourself each day aloud or in your head. It will be more potent if you say it out loud. Maybe you want to start with one and go from there. I enjoy writing little affirmations on sticky notes. I place them strategically where I will see them: a mirror, in my planner, on a doorframe, above the kitchen sink, wherever I notice them. You want to start getting these affirmations into your mind so that they can begin to work their magic!

If you want more specific affirmations related to staying strong after getting out of an abusive relationship, look at these affirmations! (Arabi, 2017):

"Every time I am silent, I protect myself against psychological violence."

The longer you keep no contact with your abuser, the more you protect yourself. As I said, narcissists are good with words. They have used their words to emotionally and psychologically abuse you over the years, making you feel *less than* and as if you are not a strong, independent person deserving unconditional love.

"I never give up; I push on."

You are not weak. You are strong. Even though the beginning part of your recovery is so so hard (I know!), you do not have to give up. You can keep pushing forward and straining toward the light and the happiness you deserve.

"I am so much stronger than empty threats."

Your abuser may try to make threats against you to get you to weaken and come back. But you are stronger than that. They only say whatever they can to get you back under their control. But you are strong.

"No one can take away what power I have inside of myself."

I love this one. People think they can break you down and mould you into whatever they want, but they cannot take what is inside of you. That is yours and yours alone.

"My will is stronger than my abuser, who tries to bully me."

Another reminder of your strength! You can do this; you can get through it no matter what your abuser tries to say to you.

"Every human being has the right to be free from abuse."

This truth is so good to remember. Abusers like to make you feel you deserve what you're getting because of who you are and your mistakes. But no way! We all deserve to be free from abuse, and you do too!

I love these affirmations because they're clear and strong, and they do not shy away from those deep fears we have inside ourselves. Another affirmation I would like to add to this list is this: "My personhood is sacred and unique, and it belongs to me."

The Habit of Meaning: Wake Up to Purposeful Life by Aligning with Your Core Values

It is naturally human to want to live a life with meaning and purpose. No matter your religious belief, we all want life to be meaningful. That's how we get through the day; that's what gives us a reason to get up in the morning, right? If we found life utterly pointless, there'd be no reason for us to do anything.

If you don't feel your life has a meaning or purpose, it's time to find one. But how? That can be difficult, especially after a codependent relationship with a narcissist. So now is the time to find yourself again and ask yourself, "What do I value?"

Your personal values are what you care deeply about. What makes you angry? What makes you cry? What are you most passionate about? Your gut reactions to the circumstances around you are significant clues to discovering the values that define your purpose and meaning. As an HSP, your intuition and ability to feel work to your advantage in finding how you can make a difference in the world.

Your values are even more important than your goals because goals are like dreams that you might not ever achieve. But it's always possible to live according to your values (Selig, 2018). Intentionally take time to develop your values; it doesn't have to be complicated. Regularly reviewing a list of your top 5 core values will help you grow and progress. Your values are your own and are a perfect example of your independence.

After you define your values, you will be able to determine your meaning and purpose in life. Once you've identified that, you can wake up each day with something to look forward to and a reason to get out of bed.

Go through the list below and highlight the words that stand out to you, the ones you think could be your core values or the ones you would like to have as core values. While there are many, keep it meaningful by observing themes in the words you are drawn to, then boil it down to between 3 and 7 core values. Then, write them as a list and order them according to their priority in your life.

Authenticity, Achievement, Adventure, Authority, Autonomy, Balance, Beauty, Boldness, Care, Comfort, Compassion, Challenge, Citizenship, Community, Competency, Contribution, Courage, Creativity, Curiosity, Determination, Entertainment, Escape, Fairness, Faith, Fame, Food, Friendships, Fun, Growth, Happiness, Health, Honesty, Hospitality, Humour, Influence, Initiative, Inner Harmony,

Integrity, Justice, Kindness, Knowledge, Leadership, Learning, Love, Loyalty, Marriage, Meaningful Work, Minimalism, Morality, Naturality, Openness, Optimism, Parenting, Peace, Physical Exercise, Pleasure, Poise, Popularity, Recognition, Religion, Reputation, Respect, Responsibility, Security, Self-Respect, Service, Simplicity, Spirituality, Stability, Success, Status, Tradition, Trustworthiness, Wealth, Wisdom, _____ (other)

Evaluate Your Life and Realign with Your Core Values

Once you have your list of the core values you would most like to live, it's time to get real with yourself by evaluating your life to consider how aligned your day-to-day thoughts and behaviours are with your list. It will be essential to recognize the discrepancies and differences so you can make changes to live more in sync with the values you selected.

Human Behaviour Specialist Dr. John Demartini provides us with 13 questions to consider as we determine our current core values. This exercise is an excellent place to begin because it helps us realistically notice our existing core values according to our actions, not our idealistic thinking. For example, we might want to think that we have a core value of living with courage but does our day-to-day behaviour support that core value? Answering these questions will require you to be very honest with yourself. If you find you have a core value you do not actually want to have, simply identifying it is the first step toward making better decisions to change and become a better version of yourself.

1. How do you fill your space?

What items are within a 4-foot radius of you at all times? Your cigarettes, phone, children, a book, a fashion item...? Consider the items you place around yourself at all times and what those items represent as it relates to your core values. For example, if it's cigarettes, it might mean a core value you have is escape. If it's your phone, it might mean your core value is beauty or creativity because you are constantly using your phone to listen to a certain kind of music, or perhaps it's growth because you are listening to self-help videos and podcasts. Being a present parent might be your core value if it's your children. Consider what that item (or person) represents to you.

2. How do you spend your time?

When you have spare time, how do you fill in the minutes? For what would you drop everything to make time? Are you watching entertaining shows or movies, reading books or articles, preparing food, taking care of your physical body, working on construction projects, hanging out with a particular person, sleeping, or doing handicrafts? What do those activities communicate about your values? (You may need to review the list of core values again in light of that activity.)

3. What energizes you?

When you get into a specific situation or topic of conversation that excites you, this is a good indication of a core value.

4. On what do you spend your money?

You wouldn't use your money for something unless you believed that item was valuable and worth the cost. So, where your finances are focused will say a lot about where your true values lay (whether you like what that is or not).

5. Where are you most organized and ordered?

Is it your music collection, books, outdoor gear, makeup, planning events...the spice rack? Consider where it seems effortless for you to organize and what that communicates about what you are valuing.

6. Where are you most disciplined & reliable?

Do you attend church regularly, every Sunday? Is it your workout routine every morning? Perhaps you are meticulous in maintaining the order of your home or personal hygiene, or you prudently put money aside in your savings account. Others may find it hard to do this, but you have made it an effortless habit in your life.

7. What do you think about most?

Maybe you are always thinking about the next thing to purchase or create to make your home more beautiful. Perhaps your thoughts always concern your children and how you can better parent them. Or do your thoughts drift to the past, to situations you long for or regret? Consider why you think about those things and what core value aligns with that reason.

8. What do you visualize most?

In your mind, what memories are you relishing, what scenes are you replaying, what dreams are you pondering, or what fantasies are you creating? What do these tell you about your focus and values?

9. What do you have an internal dialogue about most?

What conversations are you having with yourself? What topic are you most often revisiting in your mind?

10. What do you converse with other people about most?

If you are unsure, ask your friends and family the topics with which they associate you.

11. What inspires you most?

Your eyes get teary when you think about this inspiring thing because it means so much to you.

12. What are your three most consistent goals?

Through your life seasons, what themes come across when you think about what you have been striving to accomplish?

13. What do you love to learn about?

The topics in which you are passionate about expanding your knowledge and understanding are excellent indicators of your core values.

As you have been reading, I'm sure I've sparked some thoughts. Take some time to pause before moving on to the next chapter. Go through the 13 questions and core value list. It will be an enlightening and challenging exercise, and if you take it seriously, it could change the trajectory of your future.

Summary

Your new life begins as soon as you set yourself free from the old, abusive relationship. It can be easy to keep a fixed mindset about it, believing you will never grow, change, or find new relationships. But look through the lens of gratitude and arm yourself with that machete to cut down the lies and break a new path forward. Shift to the growth mindset, evaluating your core values and believing in the possibility of a bright future full of meaning. You will bounce back after hardship. In this chapter, we considered the following:

- How to practice gratitude amid grief
- The power of positive affirmations to cut a new path forward
- The core values we idealize and the ones we are currently prioritizing.

By developing the internal habits discussed above, you put the past behind you and plant new seeds that will germinate, take root and bear good external fruit later down the road. In the next chapter, we will continue looking at healthy habits, focusing more on our extroverted expression of self.

Review on Amazon.com

NARCISSISTIC ABUSE RECOVERY

Review on Amazon.co.uk

Review on Amazon.ca

Extroverted Healing Habits

WE WILL NOW BEGIN to turn our focus from deep within ourselves, swivelling toward our external world and how we show up and conduct ourselves there through our physical presence, actions and behaviours, and relationships with others. We must start with the habit of being mindful because it is the practice of being simultaneously aware of your inner world (your introverted self) and your experience in the outside world (your extroverted self). From there, we will examine the habits of self-care, authenticity, and connection.

The Habit of Mindfulness: Ground Yourself in the Present Moment

Mindfulness is putting yourself in the present, forgetting the past, not thinking about the future, and just savouring the moment.

Because narcissistic abuse creates an atmosphere where you feel less aware of who you are and what's happening, mindfulness can be especially beneficial. When you take time to ground yourself in the present and focus on mindfulness, you're recreating that inner world. As HSPs, our inner world is so much more vivid than non-HSPs. We have a greater connection to our inner selves. It's unique, but we lose it when faced with the onslaught of abuse from a narcissist.

Return to this inner world with mindfulness practice. Create a form of conscious awareness within yourself in which you can explore your thoughts and emotions. Through this practice, you can regain that sacred connection to yourself, and slowly, over time, it will help to throw off the bonds of narcissistic abuse (Hu, 2020).

Here are a few ways you can work on mindfulness in your day-to-day life:

Meditation! Spend a little time each day being quiet with yourself. Allow the thoughts and feelings to pass through you without judgment. Watch over them;

observe; learn about yourself. I find walking through my neighbourhood to be a very meditative practice. As I walk, my mind wanders and then, as I take an objective and neutral step back from my inner world, I notice the patterns and themes of my thinking.

Pausing/Check-Ins. Throughout the day, take a moment to ground yourself. Think, "I'm here, right now. How am I feeling? What am I doing?" Keep practising, and the more natural it will be. Focus on the present, and everything else just falls away. After spending extended time with others or experiencing something emotionally significant or traumatic, when I am sinking deep into my thoughts and feelings, I need this check-in moment to grip myself in reality. Usually, it's in the car on the way home.

Breathing Exercises. Some people love to engage in breathing exercises. It's a form of meditation, but it gives you something physical to do while observing your wandering mind. I personally enjoy the 4-2-7 breathing exercise, in which I breathe in for 4 seconds, hold my breath for 2 seconds, and then breathe out slowly for 7 seconds. I feel a lot more relaxed and aware of my body and feelings after repeating this for seven cycles or so. There are many tools for breathing exercises online; find one that works for you!

I struggle to prioritize mindfulness because I find I like to fill up the silence with music or YouTube videos or children. Before I left the abuse, I would get very emotional while folding laundry. I think it was because it was one of the only activities I would do mindfully and in silence. In that quiet moment, while my hands were busy, my emotions were finally able to catch up to me. My intuition and gut feelings were trying to get my attention to tell me something was very wrong in my life. I believe we need stillness and quiet to make a good evaluation of our state of being. If we don't make time for ourselves and we shut out our thoughts and feelings with constant noise or activity, it shouldn't be surprising when we later find ourselves in a place we never wanted to be. But if we regularly make space for ourselves to pay attention and listen to our needs truly, we will be able to hear when our inner voice pleads with us.

Getting quiet and observing our thoughts can feel very uncomfortable if we are not used to doing so. Give yourself time. Notice your discomfort. Tell yourself it's okay to feel uncomfortable in silence. And keep working at it.

The Habit of Authenticity: Give Voice and Action to Your Desires

A narcissist lives a life based on lies. They lie to themselves, to others, and to you. They build a facade they actually believe in. These facades make them feel all-powerful and without fault. They can get what they want out of life and don't have to face any inner darkness or demons. When you're in a relationship with a narcissist, they train you to believe in their lies.

You are told you are less than others in some fashion, and you are told they are better. They are the ones who control everything, and they are wiser, more intelligent, more attractive, and better-equipped to handle things than you are. They also lie to you, saying they are more deserving of good things than you are. They also tell you you do not deserve good things because there is some fault with you.

But if you're reading this book, you're free of the abusive relationship, so now it's time to throw off the lies and start living your authentic, best life. You've spent long enough trying to live up to whatever impossible standard the narcissist abuser in your life has set for you. It's time to focus on you, what you want, and who you are in your most authentic form.

Some say the greatest freedom is being true to oneself because it's not hinged on anyone else's opinions and gives up worry and stress that you do not please somebody else. But when you're still reeling from a relationship filled with abuse, you might not understand what being true to yourself means.

A few tips from *Mind Her Way* (n.d.) on how to live authentically include:

Do things that make you happy: HSPs especially are guilty of being major people-pleasers. Because we notice all the little ways people show us their pleasure/displeasure, we partially feel obligated to make people happy. This can be incredibly worsened after narcissistic abuse. But how about you finally switch it around? Start turning towards yourself and thinking about what makes you happy. What gives you joy? Doing those things is authenticity right there.

Avoid negativity: It's impossible to completely remove all negative influences in your life because they are everywhere, around every corner. But be mindful of what negative influences are already in your life, and consider how to avoid them. Maybe it's a certain person (besides the abuser), a particular group or place or even an activity, such as watching the News, bringing negativity to your life. What's the point? Life is hard enough without making it worse with a negative influence, especially a negative person.

Learn to say no: Later, we'll cover this in more detail when I share with you about building boundaries, but basically, it's essential to know when to say "no." Being authentic is about doing what you feel comfortable with and aligning with your values. Don't deny your true self by people-pleasing (as HSPs are wont to do!) or doing things that break your boundaries because someone might be upset if you don't. Saying "no" when you want to means listening to yourself and your desires. No longer are you putting those needs and wants down or treating them as less than, like your abuser did.

I kept my social circle very tight when I was in "the thick" of my recovery. Small talk with others can be incredibly challenging when you're grieving and struggling to make a new beginning in your life. People will ask seemingly simple questions, and you may not have simple answers to give in return. Each little interaction can be a painfully awkward reminder of the broken, messy state of your life (don't worry, it won't be like this forever!). So I avoided large social gatherings where I would be forced into uncomfortable small talk. Instead, I spent much more time alone, with my family and oldest, safest friends. I watched comedy sketches online, experimented with watercolours, and blared music while jumping on my rebounder. I read books, walked in the sunshine, baked cookies and painted my nails. I learned to enjoy my own company and that of a few select people until I felt ready to make new connections (we'll talk more about that later).

Give yourself time: This is about self-care and listening to your body and heart. It takes time to grow, evolve, and recover. Whatever you want in life takes time and process, and that's okay! So give yourself this time. Don't push yourself beyond what you can take. Also, take the time to relax, laugh, take care of your body, and have fun. That can do wonders!

I challenge you to consider your current circumstances and prioritize authenticity by identifying a current source of negativity and discomfort. Then, permit yourself to say "no" to that thing so you can give a "yes" to yourself. Think about what saying "yes" to yourself looks like right now in that specific situation.

The Habit of Self-Care: Prioritize Caring for Self to Optimize Ability to Care for Others

Honestly, HSPs aren't great at caring for themselves. Since we feel everyone's emotions, we get exhausted quickly because we often want to help and fix their problems. Because of the discomfort of our empathy (feeling others' negative emotions), we also want to make people happy and please them. We might believe taking care of ourselves is selfish since it pushes others' needs away.

Guess what? It's not selfish to care for yourself and respect your limits and boundaries. Let me repeat: It's not selfish to take care of yourself! Aren't you tired of getting burned out after caring for everyone else and feeling everything around you so deeply? Aren't you tired from all you had to deal with in your abusive relationship? Aren't you ready to start thinking about just you and what you want?

If you answered yes, that doesn't mean you're selfish. It means you are normal, and it means you're human! We mortals weren't designed to do things endlessly without physical and mental breaks. So even though you might sometimes feel like you have a strange superpower as an HSP, you're still human too! So take a break and start thinking about self-care on your recovery journey.

Think of it this way: by being at your best, after taking care of yourself, you can return to caring for others. You can be your helpful, loving, compassionate, caring self even better because you're showing that same love, help, compassion, and care to yourself (Messerschmidt, 2020).

You might not have a clue about how to take care of yourself after taking care of others for so long, so I'll give you some ideas on where to start. In my own life, I found these to be incredibly helpful. The more I cared for myself, the easier it was to make progress and take those slow steps toward the recovery I desperately wanted.

First of all, sleep! Please, please, put sleep as one of your top priorities. This is the most obvious way for your body to recharge after a long day of all that feeling and thinking. Because your nervous system is constantly running, you might need more sleep than others as an HSP. So make it a priority, and get the right amount of sleep you need!

At the beginning of my recovery, on the days when I was free from the responsibility of watching my children or going to work, I was physically unable to do more than sleep. I would get terrible migraines as my body rebelled against me and told me to shut everything down to just rest. It's much easier and better to prioritize your sleep so your body doesn't force you to take a break.

Along those lines, how can you take care of your holistic self? I mean, think of yourself, your body, your emotions, and your mind as collective systems that may need maintenance: your muscles, your bones, your digestive system, your skin, your mind, and even your emotional state. You take a holistic approach when you get a massage, go to the chiropractor, or start acupuncture. Perhaps you've never taken advantage of your work benefits package. Often counselling, therapy and coaching are paid for through the Employee Assistance Program (EAP) that many workplace benefits packages include. When was the last time you got a Physical or had your bloodwork examined by a doctor to ensure you were in good health? Have you been ignoring a physical issue like a lump or even something minor such as a wart? Pick up the phone, make the appointment and deal with it! How about a spa day? You deserve it!

Next, consider your individual body parts. Starting at the top of your body at your head, move downward and outward, considering how you can love and take care of each part of your body. (If you can afford it, go ahead and spend some money on yourself. If you are low on financial resources, consider creative alternatives.) Prepare yourself! This way of making a list is such a fun way to brainstorm. I have suggested a few things, but you will undoubtedly think of more.

Start at the top with your hair. Consider getting a fresh new cut, style and colour, or even just a trim to freshen it up. Or you might spend a few extra dollars on a higher-quality shampoo next time or a hair mask treatment.

At the top of your body also is your brain. Consider taking a class to learn something new or pick up a book to occupy your mind.

Move down to your eyes. Treat your eyes by taking in some beautiful views. Go for a nature hike or see a movie, even if you have to go alone. Or declutter the pile of papers on your kitchen table, so you don't have to look at them!

Moving outward to your ears, how can you love your ears? Consider adorning them with a new pair of earrings. Put on some music that makes you feel good, or make time to listen to your cat purr.

Your nose. Light some scented candles in your home. For some aromatherapy, you can diffuse essential oils or apply them topically. Alternatively, you can use the special-occasion-only perfume or cologne hiding in the back of your collection.

Your mouth. Get fancy and put on some lip colour! Whiten your teeth or go for cleaning at your dental office. Treat yourself to your favourite food at a restaurant or order in if you don't want to go out alone.

How about your neck? Maybe it's time for a new necklace. (You might want to do some online shopping to begin replacing all the jewellery given to you by your ex.)

Next, perhaps start a short and easy weight routine at home to define the muscles in your arms. Have you been putting off that tattoo you wanted? Too permanent? Try a pretty henna design or a temporary tattoo just for fun!

Continuing outward, consider your fingers and nails. Go ahead and get a manicure or buy a new colour polish to apply at home.

Considering your chest/breasts and lower, you might decide it's time to update your undergarment collection or ditch your sweats and invest in actual high-quality silk, cotton or flannel pajamas.

Think about your heart. Maybe it's time for a heart-to-heart with someone close to you that you've not spoken with for a while. Please pick up the phone and give them a call!

For your legs, you may decide to exercise them by walking or going for a bike ride. Or maybe it's just been a long time since you shaved.

And for your feet and toes, consider a good foot massage/soak/scrub and home pedicure or head to the nail salon to have someone do it for you. Perhaps you just need to take your shoes and socks off outside and do some grounding to feel the earth beneath you.

It would be difficult for a Highly Sensitive Person who hasn't been through abuse to be centred and focused on themselves, even though they have a rich inner life. But for you, an HSP who has gone through narcissistic abuse, you have been ripped away from your identity. So going out (or staying in!) and spending time with yourself can be a way of self-care and a path back to your old self again (Andersen, 2018).

If you feel too busy to do anything I just listed, this is a flashing neon sign that practicing self-care needs to become a higher priority in your life. So before moving on to the next habit, choose one way you can practice self-care and commit to doing it within the next 24 hours.

The Habit of Connection: Seek Out Intentional Relationships

In this final habit for healing, I want you to start focusing on collecting (or reviving) new, healthy relationships and being entirely intentional about them. When you are recovering from an abusive relationship, it's essential to avoid getting into the same dangerous situation again. It's very common for abuse victims to go through a succession of abusive relationships; it becomes a vicious cycle. I do not want that for you. I want you to break free from those unhealthy ties to abuse and find new, healthy relationships that build you up instead of tearing you down in all areas of your life.

As you enter the world again after your relationship, you might be slightly jittery about finding new connections. You might also feel entirely unsure of yourself or unworthy like no one would want to be in a relationship with you. Remember: these are all lies planted by your narcissist abuser. It may take time to let go of these lies, but know that you are worthy and valuable, and you can find new, healthy relationships in your life.

As you come into contact with new people, be intentional about how you interact with them. You need connection, as all humans do, and meeting new people is a brilliant way to continue your inner healing. But not everyone needs to be your friend, nor do you have to accept everyone as your friend. Keep your eyes peeled for people who can be a good influence on you and bring positivity to your life. As you start to make new friendships and possibly even start a new romantic relationship, consider these questions:

Does this person listen to me?

Do they have time and interest in hearing what I have to say?

Does this person show compassion and empathy toward others?

Does this person make me feel good when I'm around them?

Does this person have other close friendships besides me?

Does this person encourage me in my own life and independence?

By asking yourself questions as you get into new relationships, you are being intentional about having healthier, happier partnerships. You are both protecting yourself from future hurt/abuse and taking back control over whom you choose to bring into your life. Now that's power.

Summary

How we show up in the world as healthy HSPs is a beautiful thing, often inspiring others. In this chapter, we looked at our externally focused habits. We learned:

- How and why to ground ourselves in the present moment through mindfulness

- What it means to say "yes" to ourselves in order to live authentically

- How, practically, to care for ourselves so we can show up best for others

- We need to be intentional about whom we connect with relationally.

Next, I want to focus further on the area of connections. We will contrast signs of a healthy and harmful relationship so you'll know what to watch for. We'll look at signs of a toxic relationship so you'll know when to run to the hills. We'll also identify the very essence of healthy love so you can open yourself and be vulnerable to it. We will consider who in your circle is harmful to you and what to do about it. Finally, we'll look at what it takes to build new friendships. Ready? Let's go!

Part Three: Curate Good Relationships

Cull Connections and Recognize Toxicity

It can take years of abuse before you are ready to leave the narcissist. During that time, you will have built a life with your abuser, and once you finally leave the narc (or they leave you), you may find your whole world crumbling to pieces. After any breakup, your current social group can be in a quandary. Some people might be on your ex's side, while others might be on your side. Sometimes, the whole group will choose one person, and then you're on your own. It can make you feel incredibly lonely and lost; it's not a good time to feel that way. You might dread asking or telling a mutual friend you need them to pick your side if they want to continue a friendship with you. So, after the breakup, you're likely on the hunt for safe friends and new connections. You're looking for a support group and a fresh start.

Let's say that some people in your old group seem neutral and refuse to pick a side. That may seem reasonable enough, but for your emotional security, it may be beneficial to part ways with these friends. Let me explain. The narcissist wears his mask and plays a role so comfortably that it seems this facade is his true identity to almost everyone. Your mutual connections may not believe your story if you tell them the unmasked version of the narcissist because their experience of him will be so unlike yours. Suppose they were acquainted with the narcissist before you were. In that case, they are likely to question the reality you are presenting to them when you explain your experience of being abused and mistreated. Worse, they may try to act as a go-between you and your ex. This is a very dangerous situation because the narcissist can use your mutual friends to continue manipulating and controlling you. In addition, those friends may be giving the narcissist private information about you, even unknowingly, which the narcissist will use to your disadvantage. Finally, though they might mean well, those friends keep you tied to your ex through updates and communication, and they might even encourage you to get back with this person. None of that is healthy or helpful, and you must quickly cull those connections.

CULL CONNECTIONS AND RECOGNIZE... 113

Think back to Tabitha. After she left Derrick, she had to say goodbye to a lot of the friends they had together. At first, she thought she might be able to keep those connections. However, these people started nagging her about Derrick, questioning her decision, and making her feel guilty. Some hinted it might be too late for her to find someone else, even saying she was too old to get into another relationship. Some people reported how she was doing to Derrick and told her all about him as well. While they might have given her pleasure in the past, these relationships were now entirely unhealthy. Tabitha was on her way to recovery, and these relationships were holding her back. She needed to remove them from her life to start fresh.

I encourage you to evaluate your social circle to clarify your relationships and decide which ones are worth taking with you into your narcissist-free future.

Choose Not to Be Confused

In this season of your life, many things are hard and painful. You've done the most challenging part by ending the relationship with your abuser. Afterward, you might have also decided to move, change jobs, remove social media accounts, etcetera, to go "no-contact" and free yourself from the cycle of abuse. Since you have let go of so many things already, the last thing you want to do is end friendships, even if they have the potential to harm you and hinder your forward motion.

The *New York Times* bestselling author of *Blue Like Jazz* and creator of *Business Made Simple*, Donald Miller, shares a story and quote I connected with recently. Relating to business, Miller champions the idea that "clarity will always win the day." I suggest the same goes for relationships when recovering from narcissistic abuse.

Evaluating relationships tends to be the most excruciating part of a breakup (especially for us HSPs!). Because of the resulting pain of ending relationships, it'll be tempting to keep people around when it would be best to let them go. You might have a little *confusion* about this, mainly because you don't want to hurt or offend anyone.

Let me explain further. Donald Miller discusses a scenario when he approached his mentor, Doug Keim, about a distressing business situation he found confusing. Keim encouraged him by saying, "Don, don't choose to be confused about something that isn't confusing."

Miller unpacks this idea for his business audience by describing a scenario in which a business owner deals with a particular customer who has a lot of money and provides a lot of revenue to the company. However, dealing with this customer is always complicated. They are hard to reach, unreliable in paying their bills on time, and the company is constantly hounding them to pay invoices. The business owner might experience confusion about keeping the customer because they don't want to miss out on the revenue. But dealing with the person causes extra stress and work for everyone.

The reality is that it's time to let that client go. In their place, another customer or multiple customers can replace the lost revenue, reducing the stress and extra work for the company. Voila! Sounds simple, right? On paper, it does sound straightforward, but when you're involved emotionally in a situation, it can be oh so difficult to make the healthy decision to cut somebody loose.

After your breakup, you may feel the same "confusion" about cutting out friendships associated with your narcissistic abuser. Highly sensitive people form deep, meaningful and empathetic bonds with their friends. But if we keep ties with those connected to our abuser, we very well might be keeping ourselves vulnerable to more hurt and pain. It can feel like the most challenging thing to remove those connections from our lives, so instead, we "choose to be confused." We must objectively step back and take our emotions and empathy out of the equation. Then, it's simple to recognize the unfortunate truth that we are recovering from narcissistic abuse. Therefore, the right action to take is whatever is necessary to protect ourselves from falling back into the hands of the narcissist. This means surrounding ourselves with only safe people who genuinely understand our vulnerability and who will support us as we rebuild our lives.

If a relationship is likely to hurt you or is already causing distress, it's time to let go and move on with your life. Donald Miller makes it easier for us by providing a statement template to help reduce our confusion.

It goes like this:

> *The unfortunate truth about the situation is _____. Therefore, the right action to take is _____.*

When you fill in these blanks, it can give you incredible clarity about what to do with those friends who are liable to cause you harm. It's clear, concise, and very to the point. There is no wiggle room or chance for confusion to cloud your mind.

Think about a friend connected to your abuser, a relationship that might not be the healthiest for you and fill in the blanks of the first sentence. What is the "right action" to free you from "the unfortunate truth"?

Consider these two examples to help get you started:

> *The unfortunate truth about my friendship with Amy is that she doesn't recognize the toxicity of my narcissist ex, and as a mutual friend, she is a bridge between him and me. Therefore, the right action is to keep Amy at a distance so that my ex cannot abuse me through her.*

Here's another one.

> *The unfortunate truth about Bill and Stephanie is that they have decided to remain neutral and won't choose me over my abuser, but I need close friends who understand entirely and validate the abuse I went through. Therefore, the right action is to end my friendship with Bill and Stephanie and seek supportive companions.*

With these statements, you gain clarity about your relationships and which ones need to be removed from your life so you can heal.

Building a new life free from the narcissist will require the boldness of leaving certain relationships behind and the tenacity to create new social networks. You'll need to evaluate your current social circle and get clear about your connections to decide which friends to take with you in your new life after narcissistic abuse.

Signs of a Toxic Relationship

Next, we will discuss the signs of toxic and unhealthy relationships. As we do, I want you to consider the people you spend the most time with; your friends, family members and, if you have one, your new romantic partner. You might have heard the term "toxic relationship" before, and it sounds awful, but what does it really mean? Synonyms for the word "toxic" are "poisonous," "noxious," "injurious," "dangerous," and "malignant." It's more than just bad. A toxic relationship will repeatedly hurt you and keep you from living a happy, healthy life. Healthy relationships support our growth and development, but a toxic one will infiltrate the sacred space of your personhood with the sole intent of dismantling and tearing you down.

Getting rid of these relationships is crucial, but we can get caught up in them often. It is easy; it is common, but it's time for us HSPs to start taking more control of whom we let into our lives. It's time for us to stop feeling bad or guilty about being selective and intentional. Before discussing toxic relationships further, let's narrow down a few fundamental truths. Consider making these daily verbal affirmations to say to yourself or write them down in a visible place to refute the constant flow of lies you are tempted to believe.

"I am deserving of friendship."

"I am worthy of love."

"There are high-quality individuals who would enjoy being my friend or partner."

"I have the capacity to be a good friend and partner."

Say these a few times to yourself regularly if you need to. HSPs who have been through narcissistic abuse struggle with these basic truths more than others. That's why it's so easy for HSPs to fall back into abusive partnerships, tolerate toxic behaviours, and regress in their healing after escaping the former relationship. You need to grab hold of these truths. Sure, you are hurting and grieving, and your abuser mixed things up in your head so much you don't recognize your value anymore. But if you change your thinking by saying and believing these statements, you will begin to attract healthier relationships. Fake it 'til you make it if you have to. Just start telling yourself these things, and it will go a long way to helping you see when a relationship is just no good and far less than what you deserve.

But what are some key ways to know when a relationship is toxic? Here are some tell-tale signs.

You feel drained. You put all your effort into keeping the relationship alive but never feel filled up in return.

Nothing ever seems to be the other person's fault. Whether with you or someone else, the person in this relationship never believes they have done something wrong. They avoid personal responsibility and consistently blame others, including you!

Things are too intense, too fast. Intensity right at the beginning of a new relationship and over-the-top behaviour is unusual and a sign something isn't quite right. It can lead to a strange control and obsession (10 Signs of an Unhealthy Relationship, n.d.).

You don't feel safe sharing your feelings or approaching them with difficult subjects. Safety in relationships is enormous! It's everything! If you don't feel safe talking with this friend, then it's not a good relationship.

You feel diminished after interactions with the person. Over time, your confidence erodes in this kind of relationship, and you don't feel supported, loved, or even respected. Get out of there!

A relationship shouldn't be taking more from you than it gives. Of course, you have experience with this after having gone through an abusive partnership, but the more you know about toxic relationships, the better you can avoid them in the future. Essentially, it boils down to this: A toxic person will always put themselves first, and they will not provide the usual beneficial aspects of friendship/partnership like love, kindness, acceptance, etc. A toxic relationship is not what you need right now or ever. Believe in yourself: You deserve better and more!

After leaving the narcissist, when you find and are interested in someone new, you'll want to be more cautious and intentional about forming a bond. Here are some questions (Steber, 2019) to help evaluate a potential romantic partner.

How often do I feel doubt, anxiety, and discomfort in this relationship? If you're feeling these often, that's a big sign you should run for the hills.

Is this relationship exactly like all my past relationships? Check for negative patterns that keep cropping up. If you feel the same as you felt during the relationship with your abuser, then it's goodbye time.

Do I feel safe and cared for? Is there love and support? Or do you still feel emotionally abused, controlled, or not thought worthy or valuable?

Is my relationship holding me back? Do I feel like I can't take steps towards a better, bright future after my breakup because of this relationship?

Do we have a similar approach to life? Similarities within our relationships can give us great comfort and support. How similar are you?

Am I happy? This may seem too basic, but as HSPs, we often forget our happiness because others' unhappiness weighs on us greatly. So, check in with your feelings to see if it's time to say goodbye.

If you answered these questions, and the outcome is negative, then you have your answer. You can "choose not to be confused" and begin to cull the unhealthy connections and relationships in your life.

Conclusion

Throughout my recovery, it's been challenging to believe in myself and accept that I deserve deep friendships and a romantic partner who will truly cherish and support me. My abuser had isolated me from others, and I struggled to maintain quality friendships during the years we were together. After I was free from him, I found myself grieving as I made new friendships. I finally realized I had been missing out on the joy of deep friendship connections the entire time I was with him. The richness of company and community is a beautiful thing. No one person can meet every need that we have. In the variety of our friends, we see the many different sides of ourselves, so I felt like I came alive again when I spent time with new friends. These people loved and gave back to me, asked me questions, checked in to see how I was doing, and participated in a reciprocal relationship. This had been foreign to me for years because of the isolation I had gone through. Unconsciously, I adopted a belief of unworthiness because of my experience. But all that has changed now.

I want you to know you are worthy of good relationships. You deserve happiness and love and to experience the joy life can bring with other people. Don't hide away from it. There is such peace and happiness in friendships and partnerships, and I want you to find it again. So, choose not to be confused about toxic relationships. They only keep you from who you could be and what you could have, so take steps to cut them out of your life. I know it'll be hard; I know exactly how you feel about saying goodbye to people you thought were your friends. But to get better, you must root out the toxicity and remaining poison in your life. Let the healing begin.

Summary

This chapter was about understanding toxic relationships and how you can choose not to be confused when it's time to cull your connections.

- If a relationship isn't reciprocal and doesn't provide you with love, support, safety, and guidance, then it could be time to let it go!

- Choose not to be confused about what to do when dealing with a toxic person and those who connect you back to that person in an unhealthy way.

- Spot the toxic person/relationship and break the connection. Avoid this type of person in the future.

- Take courage and strength!

In the next chapter, we'll see the difference between healthy and unhealthy love and consider how to look for new friends in your life. Healthy, helpful friendships are the glue that holds you together during dark times. So, bring on healthy love!

Make New Friends and Recognize Healthy Love

I DO NOT WANT this book to sound like a children's television show teaching you how to make friends in a cheesy, sing-song way. We're no longer children, and that fact can be a hindrance when it comes to making friends. When my children play at the park, they walk straight up to other kids and simply ask, "do you want to be my friend?" or "do you want to play with me?" The return answer is almost always "yes," and away they go! Children are great at making friends. But it feels strange to make friends as an adult. It's almost like you're reverting to your childhood self, and you experience all the insecurity and awkwardness that comes with it.

Tabitha was in a marriage that lasted for years with a narcissistic abuser. Derrick took control of everyone she spoke to and saw during that time. Like all narcissists, Derrick wanted to be Tabitha's everything, so he carefully manipulated her to cut ties with people or only see those he approved. Whenever Tabitha tried to go out with her friends or call someone on the phone, Derrick made her pay the price. He gave her the silent treatment, outright yelled at her or picked a fight so she would be anxious or in distress immediately before or after her interaction with other people.

Over time this abusive action affected Tabitha's mental state and confidence and took away her power to maintain relationships with anyone other than Derrick. Once free of him and the abusive marriage, she decided to make new friends again. But imagine her fear and uncertainty! For so long, Derrick controlled whom she could see and with whom she could interact. For so long, she felt unworthy of real love and believed she deserved whatever lousy treatment she received! Everything felt foreign, unfamiliar, and uncomfortable when she attempted to regain control of her friendships.

If you can relate to Tabitha, know that you're not on your own. I know what you feel like; many abuse survivors have had to walk this road. But there is hope! Making new and wonderful friends who can be your support system is possible. One of the most important things you need going forward is to know the difference between healthy and unhealthy love.

How to Make Friends: The High-Value How-To Guide

Making friends when we were young used to be as easy as, "Hey, you're my neighbour, and you're my age, so let's be friends!" If you have an introverted or reserved personality like me, a few guidelines on where to start when making new friends can give you strength and courage when everything feels chaotic. As an adult, "it's hard to find a friend," as that Tom Petty song says. But if your "days are going by like paper in the wind," don't get overwhelmed. These ideas can guide you—no need to do all of them at once; just start somewhere. (Vogel, 2022):

Take the initiative: This is the uncomfortable part about making friends after you leave an abusive situation. Making friends takes effort, and you need to put in the work. Taking the initiative is making the opening move and going out of your way to talk to new people. Make that first step, which is so hard for HSPs, if you want to start taking control to have the friendships you want. Just start practicing. When you find yourself in line at the grocery store, at the park with other parents or at the till ready to pay for a meal or merchandise, make an opening move to strike up a conversation. Say something about the weather, ask them how their day is going or give them a sincere compliment. Even if the person does not reciprocate your friendliness, you'll be stretching and growing your comfort level.

Get involved and join something: This is what adults do. It's like the playground for grownups! Start with something small if you're feeling too nervous about going big. Maybe you go to a lecture or join an online book club. You can start with one group or join a couple. Get involved with a sports team or a volunteer group. There are tons of options these days! The more you get involved and out of the house, the more likely you will meet new and exciting people with friendship potential.

Show that you're receptive and open to friendship: People go off vibes, big time. You'll get what you ask if you're putting out a don't-talk-to-me vibe. Pay attention and be mindful of your body language. Turn your body toward people and look them in the eyes. Don't close yourself off by crossing your arms over your body. Instead, put out the vibe that you're interested in having friends and when people speak to you, be friendly!

Smile: Smiling makes a huge difference. Would you want to talk to someone or seek out their friendship if they never smiled and looked sour all the time? Of course not! Smile, even if you're not feeling confident, happy, or particularly friendly, you'll still be putting out the good vibes.

Be a good listener: To find a friend, be a friend. You know what it's like to go unheard and have your feelings unexplored by others. Be a good listener to the new people you're meeting, and show that you care. Show your ability to be a good friend by asking questions and listening attentively to each answer. People will feel you respect them, which will go a long way to make them feel valued.

Network: Invite people you already know to act as access points for new friendships. A colleague, mentor, or long-time friend can make connections for you, bringing you one step closer to finding new friends when they introduce you to someone in their circle. This can be a safe place to start in the aftermath of abuse. Look for and grab hold of all the opportunities you can to discover friends!

Be consistent: This is part of being a good friend. If you're beginning a relationship with some new people, be sure to respond to their contact, show up when they invite you to things and be reliable. People will stop contacting you if you are unresponsive or push them away. It's just a fact.

Don't put everything on one person: When you experience that empty vessel feeling, you want to fill it instantly. But be careful not to have unrealistically high expectations of people. You might put too much responsibility on these new people to make you feel better in your time of grief. Hold back on that. Friendships are lovely and can be incredibly supportive, but do not foster co-dependency by using people as crutches. You still need to do the work inside yourself during your healing process, and by putting too much on one person, you can lose them.

The more you put yourself out there to explore places where you have opportunities to meet new people and try new things, the better chance you'll have at finding more friends. Having a good variety of friendships will lead to greater confidence in yourself because you'll see what you have to offer in other people's eyes. Being many things to many people will go a very long way in healing from your wounds and moving you forward to a brilliant future.

Unhealthy Love vs. Healthy Love (Romantic Love)

I used to think romantic love was an upbeat and euphoric state that couldn't be wrong. Since we see and hear about it everywhere in our culture, through songs, movies, and books, we idealize the concept. Society influences us from childhood to focus and strive toward positioning ourselves in romance. It's like we can't escape it. I remember growing up oblivious to the concept that there is healthy love and unhealthy love. Since love is subjective and has many facets and complexities, it often takes an objective outsider's point of view to realize a partner is injuring you.

As HSPs, we feel the emotion of love right down to our core. Whether for friends, family, or a romantic partner, our passion is always strong. We have a more extraordinary instinct for love than the average person, in terms of how we feel and give to others. This doesn't make us better or worse; it is only because we have a deep understanding of emotions. For an HSP, we are never very far from our various emotions. We tap into them constantly. Therefore, when someone we love deeply hurts us, we feel that hurt like nothing else. But it can still be hard to turn away from that relationship because of how much we love.

Our depth of feeling makes it easier to accept unhealthy love when we deserve so much more. Therefore, it's important to arm ourselves with the knowledge of what we deserve and help ourselves avoid future pitfalls. So, what is healthy love?

This question can be complicated to answer if you grew up in an abusive household or didn't have the chance to observe good, healthy love first-hand. So here are some thoughts to gauge what healthy love is and what a positive relationship ought to look like.

You listen and hear each other: In unhealthy love, one or both people don't listen to the other. For the non-listener, the conversation is a selfish experience void of care for the other person. Healthy love is all about paying attention. In healthy love, each person takes turns speaking. The conversation easily flows back and forth since each person responds appropriately to what the other has just said. If someone consistently turns the conversation toward themselves, they are not practicing listening skills to flow with you in the conversation. An obvious red flag is when a person speaks for long periods without allowing an exchange of dialogue.

You feel compassion and support: For an HSP, it's more natural than not to give understanding and encouragement (sometimes too much!). So, it's imperative we receive compassion and support in return. In unhealthy love, HSPs usually give all they have without receiving any meaningful encouragement or positive affirmation in return. Healthy love is balanced.

You get that "sympathetic joy" feeling: Healthy love is about feeling good and positive when your partner is happy. Unhealthy love is when one partner feels happy at their partner's expense. A narcissist may regulate their feelings by offloading emotion onto you. You may have been happy and calm before interacting with them but you leave the conversation feeling flustered or anxious. Meanwhile, the narcissist came into the interaction with negativity and went away happy and calm, this was an unhealthy transfer of emotions. If you and your partner are happy for each other and can share positive emotions, this is healthy love.

You both believe in and respect each other's boundaries: Boundaries are foundational in relationships because they define the essence of each person! In an abusive relationship where unhealthy love abounds, the abuser will disrespect your boundaries, reject your "no," and disregard your opinions, needs and desires. But in healthy love, each person respects the other person's boundaries and strives to uphold the others' individuality. Boundaries can relate to anything: the need for alone time, commitment to church attendance, willingness for physical affection, etc. Healthy love is respecting that line. While it is your personal responsibility to set and maintain your boundaries, an exceptionally loving partner will encourage you as an HSP to define and communicate your parameters so they can accommodate your sensitivities and commit to honouring them! You are worth the extra effort! Remember, we tend to be people-pleasers, so it's easy for us to blur the line. But if your partner understands you and helps you stick to your guns, you've got a good one.

There is room for emotion: For HSPs, we need the space to feel our many emotions. We also want to be supported when we are in our feelings. A narcissist will make an HSP feel guilty for having emotions, accusing them of being "crazy," "dramatic," or "too sensitive." There is no space, freedom or encouragement to feel and, therefore, no validation of those feelings. So, we try to rein them in, which doesn't do us any good. In healthy love, there is room for emotions. We have the space to feel the myriad of emotions passing through us each day. If your partner supports you in this, they will say things like, "I'm so sorry. That must be very difficult," instead of "Buck up! It's not that bad!" This is healthy love.

Fighting isn't about being number one: In healthy love, it's a fair fight. Abusive tactics such as gaslighting, stonewalling (silence), cruelty or contempt are part and parcel of unhealthy love. In healthy love, both partners are on the same side. With maturity, they come together to face the problem, fighting against the threat to the relationship, not each other. If you can fight fair with your partner, then it's a good relationship.

You can be your true, authentic self: This is a beautiful sign of healthy love. When you don't have to walk on eggshells around your partner, trying to hide parts of yourself, or deny things you genuinely want or enjoy, this is a good sign of a healthy relationship.

Conclusion

Friendships are essential to a good and happy life. When we're suffering, we may think we don't need anybody or think people are more fuss than they're worth. After being hurt so markedly, it can be tempting to stay away from others because we don't want to feel the depth of pain and disappointment again. But you are not a hermit; you are not designed to be alone, and yes, there is always the potential for pain when we put ourselves out there, but having good friends and a devoted partner is worth the risk! So don't shy away and wallow in your loneliness during your healing and recovery time.

Many years ago, while living and travelling with people who shared my faith values, I struggled with depression and felt very alone and unsupported. I will never forget the words of a mentor when he asked me how I was (really) doing. "Lory, don't be an island," he said, "you need to build a bridge so others can reach you." The bridge from self to others, this mentor told me, is vulnerability. I've never forgotten these words and still remind myself of them from time to time. It's made all the difference.

Reach out. Be a friend. Smile. Listen. Love. Be vulnerable and show others you crave connection; relationships will come of it. I promise you will find friends who care about you and won't try to destroy your soul.

A Supportive Community of HSPs
When I was starting over again, one of the greatest needs I had was to build new connections with other people...people who were safe and kind and with whom I could share my story and take refuge. I have been very fortunate to find and be a part of a couple of different communities of friends who help me exactly like this. It took effort at first to put myself out there again but it has really paid off. Finding *your people* is one of the greatest missions you can accomplish.

I realize that many people, especially HSPs, struggle to find relational support as they are recovering from narcissistic abuse. It may be difficult to find sympathetic souls who understand what you've been through or who feel safe.

That's why I am building a private online community on Facebook. While it might not be as good as connecting with people in person, I hope it will serve to meet these very real needs. It can be a starting point so you know you are not alone as you bravely walk your recovery road. Find us at:

www.facebook.com/groups/thehighlysensitivepersonsrecovery

Summary

Love isn't just love. It can be incredibly beautiful, building us up and making life worthwhile. But, on the other hand, the unhealthy version, masquerading as love, is evil, dangerous, and toxic. It will not improve life; it will only worsen each day. So, get out there and find yourself the love you deserve with the right person and friends who appreciate that you're highly sensitive. They will do whatever it takes to help you feel loved. This chapter covered the beauty of making friends, how to do it, and the difference between healthy and unhealthy love. Remember:

- Making friends is a little more complicated as an adult, but it's not impossible.

- Put yourself out there little by little.

- Don't settle for loneliness or toxic people.

- Seek out the friends and the love you want by being open and allowing yourself to feel vulnerable.

- Unhealthy love is selfish, taking joy in a partner's pain and problems. Healthy love is an environment in which both partners feel loved and supported for who they are.

In the next chapter, we will explore the idea of finding a safe space. After abuse, our safe space has been violated—time to focus on rebuilding borders and recognizing the sacredness of it all.

Part Four: Custodian Sacred Spaces

Your Need for a Safe Space

THOSE WHO HAVE LEFT romantic relationships after narcissistic abuse must rebuild their homes. Those leaving toxic workplaces because of narcissistic bosses/co-workers must rebuild their workplace boundaries. Those cutting off relationships with narcissistic family members must guard their personal lives against exposure to those in the family who are not safe. All these situations require intentionality around creating and protecting a sacred and safe space to be authentic, to get emotional, and to take care of self. For HSPs, in particular, this is not an easy task because we don't like conflict and may not welcome change. Change brings about a whole wealth of new and difficult emotions a hurting HSP may not be ready to deal with. And conflict brings its own issues.

But I encourage you to add this to your list of fundamental truths. Every person needs a safe space to be authentic, to feel all emotions without judgment and rest from the world's craziness, to establish separateness and independence from others, and enjoy their unique personhood. I use the term "sacred" to describe this space because I believe we are all created unique and different from one another. By embracing our identity and being wholly true to ourselves, we honour our Creator.

You stand out in a crowd because of your highly sensitive nature. More than many people, you need a space you can go to escape and feel safe.

However, unless you are intentional about it, it's likely you will let others barge in and stomp all over your sacred territory. Good fences make good neighbours. It's time you build walls and gates around the garden of your life. Fence yourself in with boundaries, say "yes" to yourself, and start taking care of yourself like never before.

Building Boundaries: Why is it So Tough?

One of the aspects of an HSP is the desire for connection, which can get in the way of caring for ourselves and creating boundaries between us and others. Whether with people or just the world, we desire a deep, meaningful connection, and we will try to seek it out.

I love how Robyn Penney at HSPWorld describes HSPs as "master connectors." She states:

> "They are known for wonderful abilities to empathize, to hold space for others, and even, in moments of spiritual uplift, to feel that great, unifying force – the sense that we are but a drop in a vast ocean of universe." (Penney, 2018)

When I try to explain to others what it's like being highly sensitive, I usually say something like this: "You just feel everything." It sounds a bit vague, but it's true. The world is like this beating, thrumming thing, and highly sensitive people are attuned to everything going on around them. It's so incredibly beautiful, but it's also exhausting.

However, because of this ability and desire to connect, we let ourselves become drained without taking time out. Because we want to connect and please others, we push our needs to the wayside and say "no" to parts of ourselves that cry out for us to listen to them. And in an abusive relationship, this common HSP problem becomes even worse. We are subliminally told to deny ourselves to give to the abuser. Because of that, we forget who we really are, and that sacred protective space gets further and further away from us.

Then, after we are free from the abuse, we are like a newly born animal, struggling to stand on its fresh wobbly legs. Lost in a crazy world where we still feel all the vibrations, we can't seem to find our way home, back to ourselves. But it's time, my dear HSP friend. It's time to build boundaries around your sacred space and your beautiful self, time to take care and infuse yourself with life once again.

Boundaries for HSPs: What's a Less Limiting Term?

The idea of boundaries can sound a bit stark and harsh for highly sensitive people. We don't love sharpness, abruptness, or starkness. We hate being firm because it means we have to explain the reasons to people who might not like it. It can create conflict we didn't want or ask for, and a highly sensitive person just doesn't want to deal with that. Pleasing others and floating along where we give and give is just...easier.

Except for the fact that it's not! You're tired, used up, and exhausted. Your vampire abuser sucked you dry, consuming all the positive aspects of your highly sensitive nature. Now you're on the other side, wondering if you have anything left to give. I'm sure others besides your abuser have drained you dry, using up what you had to offer because people will do that. The HSP has many valuable and rare gifts to offer. Many will take them without thinking about the effect on the HSP.

So, HSPs may feel limited by the idea of boundaries, which force them to be a certain way, fit into a box, or create unnecessary conflict, bringing more stress into their lives. I want to turn all that around and help you understand boundaries are not limiting. They are freeing! Boundaries set you free from being at everyone's beck and call. Instead of losing yourself in others, you can stand strong and true, sparkling in the sun of your own identity. You can stop dimming your light so others can shine, stop feeling like such an outsider, and learn to appreciate all you are and have to give.

Penney (2018) describes a list of unique ways HSPs can look at boundaries to keep them from appearing too stark and harsh. Use these terms instead when thinking about creating your safe space, and keep them in mind when we discuss boundary architecture in the following chapter.

Constructing boundaries as an HSP is, first of all, protection. You are keeping yourself safe when you build boundaries. This is true for your physical self as well as your emotional/mental self. You know your limits, and by setting boundaries, you're taking a step back to keep from getting hurt or drained.

Creating boundaries is affirmation. You are recognizing and affirming whom you are and appreciating that person. You're looking at yourself and saying, "Hey, I need some time away from the world to just be." There is no judgment, and you don't have to feel guilty. You're learning to care for and love the parts of yourself that come with being highly sensitive.

Establishing boundaries is also about balance. Everyone needs balance, not just HSPs. It's the order of the universe. When part of you is off-balance, such as too much time spent feeling, something else, like action-taking or logical thinking, will suffer. That's why toxic relationships and even too much giving in healthy relationships can exhaust a highly sensitive person. Boundaries establish balance.

Creating boundaries is a sign of humility. Far be it from me to say an HSP suffers from hubris, but in a way, we do. We think our bodies, hearts, and minds can handle so much more than they really can. We push ourselves to the brink, thinking it's what we have to do. But when you establish boundaries and create a place away from everyone, you accept this fact: you can't do everything, and you need time to rest.

When you build boundaries, you are practising self-care. HSPs struggle with this idea so much! But think of boundary maintenance as a daily activity just as important as the need to take a shower or eat a good meal! Every aspect of ourselves needs boundaries to establish the care of self. Think of it this way. The more you care for yourself, the better you can care for others and maintain the connection you so crave!

Lastly, you show yourself respect, honour, and integrity when you keep your boundaries. When you are feeling well, healthy, respected, and rested, the way you show up to life and the good you can do increases exponentially. You are ready to take on the world and live in its chaos because your boundaries bolster you to withstand all its stimulation and pressure. By creating walls, fences, hedges and gates, you respect and honour yourself while encouraging others to do the same. Thus, you can live a life of integrity.

Creating a safe space for yourself does not mean you shut yourself off from the world and leave others behind. Think of it more as taking a step back, quieting the voices, or walking down a different path for a while. Then, when you're ready, you can easily return to the hustle and bustle. It's like taking a coffee break at work to be more productive. You take a coffee break (or tea time!) from life, putting a bit of distance between you and the world to check in with yourself to ensure you are safe, rested, and taken care of before returning.

I know what it sounds like, and I was reluctant to do it myself when I began my healing journey. But it has made all the difference. By periodically shutting out the noise and distractions, I'm not as exhausted; I have more energy and presence to give to others when I go out, and I have reconnected with the parts of myself my abuser tried to make me abandon. A safe space can provide you with what you've always wanted: acceptance of yourself.

Creating a Sacred Space

So, what does this actually look like in real life? Each day holds its own disarray and doesn't slow down, even if we struggle to keep up. Visiting your sacred space can be problematic in the throes of all our busyness, but it is possible. All you need is a little time; everyone has 15 minutes. It doesn't have to be every day, at least not at first, but intentionally search for the moment in your day to be in that space. If you're still thinking retreating is selfish, then stop. Selfish is pushing yourself to the limits believing you're impervious to burnout or fatigue. We're all human, and we all have our breaking points. So, take some time in your safe space before or after going out into the noisy and chaotic world.

YOUR NEED FOR A SAFE SPACE

When establishing your sacred space, find a place where you love to be. Make sure it's quiet so you won't be interrupted. Maybe it's a lonely park bench, a separate room, or even a closet in your house. Whatever it is, pick a spot where you think you could spend uninterrupted time. If you live with others, boundaries mean you'll communicate with those people that this is your sanctuary, and when you're there, they mustn't interrupt you. Then, once you have your space, put things in it you love. The whole point of a safe space is to feel calm and happy. So, what can you put in this space to make you feel calm, safe, warm, and at ease? It could be anything: a wingback chair, soft classical music, candles, throw pillows, plants, books, journals and quality pens, your cat, crochet basket or hot tea! I recommend having a whiteboard or wall space where you can post and review your daily affirmations.

It's just as essential to realize what things are not allowed in your safe space. Of course, there should be absolutely no judgment, self-loathing, or guilt. But beyond that, consider excluding physical items as well, such as no alcohol, no phones, etc. Whatever you think should be outlawed to help you hear your inner voice, and feel at ease and away from the outside world (*Valko*, 2020).

Also, consider visiting at the same time every day or every week. Even though it might be hard at first to visit your curated nook, if you schedule the appointment with yourself into your daily calendar, you'll start to look forward to it every day. You may even be running toward your sanctuary to get that much-needed rest when the clock strikes "me time."

Make the space whatever you want. In this atmosphere, recharge however you like. Of course, many people like to use prayer or meditation to recharge, but you know yourself. What gives you restored energy? What makes you feel loved, appreciated, and safe? What will build you up to help you return to the outside world feeling energized and prepared? It's up to you. As HSPs, we're used to other people telling us what to do and how to be. In this space, it's all yours and entirely under your control. So, I encourage you to make it whatever you want and need it to be.

Conclusion

Even Superman needed the Fortress of Solitude to get away from it all. A hero who could do anything, even turn back time, he still needed a place to be himself and recharge. Okay, so you're not Superman, but the heart of the idea remains. You need a space all your own, a space to just be you and forget about everyone and everything else. It is not about being selfish or forgetting other people's needs, even though others may try to tell you this. It is about giving to yourself and having that same compassion for yourself which you so often give to others. People adore all the love-giving an HSP offers them. So why not give yourself a little love too? You deserve it. I promise you the more you give to yourself, the more you set aside a space to simply be as highly sensitive as you like and enjoy and appreciate your unique personhood, the fuller and more energized you will be.

You will have so much more to give others, and a zest for life will come back in full force. The liveliness and passion I carried when I was single died during my abusive marriage. I lost my delight for life. The way back to who I was and my purpose had become blurry. My heart was not being fed or nurtured, so it slowly weakened, begging me to listen to it. Once I realized I needed to feed and nurture this integral part of myself, I became strong and whole again. Build your new world, create your boundaries, and happiness and fulfilment will overflow your heart.

Summary

This chapter focused on the mindset and initial work of boundary building, creating a physical and atmospherically safe space just for you!

- As an HSP, you need to be intentional about

your sacred territory, where you exist without judgement and feed the oft-neglected side of yourself.

- Boundaries can be a harsh term. Think of them more as protection, balance, self-care, and respect for yourself.

- Devise a place where you feel safe, calm, and away from it all. Your cozy haven is an embrace, ready to enclose and cover you whenever you desire or need it.

In the following chapters, I'll explore this idea of boundaries more deeply, fleshing it out and getting down to the quintessential. Boundaries are the way to go, my friends, and we'll start with building boundaries in your social spaces!

Building Boundaries for Others

BOUNDARIES ARE A WAY to show the world you deserve respect. It's a way to communicate with others what you like, what you want, what you need, and what you do not like or will not tolerate. Trust ensues when someone respects your boundaries. You can tell the quality of a person by the measure of how they regard and respect you. Since we posture ourselves as loving and open, we HSPs tend to welcome individuals into our lives who are not worthy of being there because they have no intention of respecting our boundaries. For the future, boundary crossing is a bright red warning sign!

After communicating the line, see how people react. Their response will help you know which people can bring support, love, and goodness to your life and which people will not. When someone disregards your boundaries, they hold you in contempt, ignoring and dishonouring the message your limits are communicating. This sort of person is undeserving of your proximity. Moreover, a person willing to respect your boundaries listens and appreciates your personhood, thus demonstrating trustworthiness. With this kind of person, you are safe to build a relationship. Only give trust in proportion to the other person's respect for your boundaries. You can relax your guard once you know someone better and they have a track record of respecting you. Keep this in mind as you establish and communicate your limits in your new life after your abusive relationship. Over time, you'll improve at keeping and communicating the boundaries you need to stay safe and happy.

Why Build Boundaries?

Many people, not just you, struggle with boundaries, which is why many relationships suffer and people get taken advantage of or steamrolled into toxic/abusive relationships (like us!)

But what benefits come from drawing and holding the line? I've been vague thus far, so let's spell it out. Keep in mind that these can apply to both platonic relationships and romantic ones.

Boundaries help avoid conflict because they establish limits. A good boundary-builder will ask: How does a person know where the line is until I show or tell them? I sometimes struggle with that idea because I generally know where an appropriate line is. I wouldn't push past it on others in a reverse scenario. But many do not care or do not think about the personal boundaries of those around them. So, in your relationships, you can avoid unnecessary conflicts by being clear about what you want. It's not about bossing someone around. It's about stating what you will and will not tolerate.

For example, when Tabitha established a new romantic relationship after Derrick, she told her new partner, "I won't tolerate the silent treatment in arguments. You need to talk things out with me if you're upset." She established a boundary in a relationship, and now her new partner knows. If he respects it, then the relationship has a chance of continuing. If he doesn't, Tabitha knows he isn't worth her time.

Boundaries can help you feel more secure about where you stand. As HSPs, we are constantly thinking about what others want. But when you begin establishing your borders, you're really thinking about what you want and no one else. When you have these boundaries in your mind, you'll start to feel less insecure in relationships because you have confidence about what you want and need, and you can share it with the other person. Relationships don't have to be a guessing game for yourself and a chance for someone to steamroll you.

Boundaries also can help you create responsibility for your actions. We are all in control of our actions, no one else's. This empowering idea means we can make the changes we want to see in ourselves and our relationships. Boundaries are taking action, and you're taking the wheel instead of letting someone else do it. For example, your narcissistic abuser might have told you, "I treat you that way because you let me treat you that way." (Maybe not in so many words.) Well, step back, Judas (like way, way back), because now, a new boundary-builder is in the house! No more receiving terrible treatment without consequence! (McMahan, 2017).

Boundaries, despite their restrictive name, are actually the way to give yourself freedom! Finally, you won't feel the weight of having to listen to other people's needs or desires over your own. Finally, you won't feel the pull of control your narcissistic partner had over you. You are now a person all your own! Establishing and keeping boundaries can give you that.

Boundaries in Social Spaces and How to Build Them

After the abuse you've experienced, it may be tricky for you to figure out what boundaries you have or want. The best way to learn more about your personal boundaries is to think about them in your social spaces, with your family, friends, and co-workers. How you interact with others and how they interact with you can help you figure out your boundaries.

Katherine Mackenzie-Smith, on the site *Highly Sensitive Refuge* (2022), states that HSPs can set boundaries, even if it feels difficult. There are multiple ways you can determine where to put the stick in the sand and judge when someone has crossed your line. Take a look at Smith's ideas about how to discover your boundaries:

Start being more conscious of where others are influencing you. People love when others do what they want, and they can push them to do it. HSPs are the perfect victims because we love people-pleasing! But as you interact with others (and get rid of those toxic relationships, remember?), start thinking about where you are tempted to give in when you should hold firm. Maybe you're saying "yes" to going somewhere when you need to rest or finish chores at home. Perhaps you're saying "yes" to having sex or getting very physical with your partner when you really don't want to. Or maybe you're taking on someone else's tasks at work because you want that person to like you and avoid conflict. Whatever it is, start compiling some research on where you see people taking advantage of you. Write these things down, and this information can direct you where to build your boundaries.

Practice saying NO. I've put the word "no" in all caps, but I don't want you to believe this word is a negative thing. Saying "no" at the right time is unbelievably healthy, mature, and confident, yet we usually only hear the negative aspects of speaking the word "no." And that's likely because people don't welcome hearing this word from others. For example, let's say your date wants to have sex with you, but you want to wait for a demonstrated long-term commitment before getting intimate, so you say, "no." Your partner may be disappointed or hurt, making you believe saying "no" is bad or wrong. Not at all! You've created a boundary and communicated it to someone else. If you say "yes" when you actually want to say "no," that is not loving yourself; you're allowing others to take control of your life. Begin looking where you have the first instinct to say "no," but you usually end up saying "yes" to keep someone happy. Follow your instincts! They're a guide to good boundaries!

Monitor your body's response to situations. As HSPs, we feel feel feel, and so our bodies are excellent indicators of our emotions. When something happens in your interactions with others, check in with your body to see if a boundary is being crossed or if one needs to be established. For example, when you hear your co-worker asking you for help again to finish one of their projects, you might feel your heart race or your cheeks getting warm. Or you might feel instantly tense or nervous. This is a sign that a boundary is getting crossed. You're unhappy about the situation and need to do something about it!

Evaluate who in your social spaces makes you feel overwhelmed. Sometimes people bring out this stress response in us, which means it could be time to set some boundaries with those people. Once you've established who those people are, think about why they overwhelm you and if it's all the time or only on certain occasions. These reflections can help you identify where your boundaries lie and where you can start building.

Strategy for Boundary Beginners!

When I had to start from scratch to build myself up again after abuse, I wanted all the clear instructions I could get. As we nervously climb out of the deep well of darkness and despair back to the light of recovery, clarity is the rope to which we cling. Now you know why boundaries are a good thing for you and how you can begin the thinking process of creating boundaries. So, it's time to get into the quintessential: the hands-on labour of actually constructing them. I want to share with you a few ideas on situations where you can build boundaries by using the powerful word "no." And these situations are oh so familiar to the struggling HSP, so I know you've been there before. This time, you'll get to look at these situations in a new light and with new competency.

These excellent ideas come from Dr. Josephine Hardman's site and her article, *How to Set Boundaries as a Highly Sensitive Person - With Scripts!* (n.d.). I won't share all the scenarios, but just a few can give you an idea of how to use your "no" in a beautiful, boundary-building way!

The First Scenario: All right, you've been here. Someone at work asks you for help, but you're overwhelmed as it is, and you can barely keep your head above water. What to do? How to say "no"? No doesn't have to be harsh and unkind; it can be polite and mannerly when you construct it the right way. If you're too busy to help someone with whatever it might be, simply say, "I'm so sorry, but my plate is full at the moment, so I won't be able to help." Or, you could say, "I'd love to help you, but I can't. Right now is a super busy time for me."

Those answers are neither unkind nor rude, but they convey the message to the other person. You're telling them "no." You've established your boundary in this scenario, and you're sticking to it. HSPs think they have endless time and energy to help everyone, but we don't. Learning when and what your limits are can be life-changing.

The Second Scenario: Someone crosses a time boundary with you. They continually arrive late when you've scheduled a time and carved out a space in your day for them. This can happen with family, friends, or co-workers and can be extremely awkward. I hate when someone makes me wait more than a few minutes, especially if I've cleared my schedule for them or they don't let me know their estimated arrival time. It's obvious they didn't make our meeting a priority as I did for them. In certain situations, it shows a complete lack of respect and a disregard for boundaries. In this situation, you have a few options for how you want to make someone know about your limitations:

"Sorry, but I have something after this for which I can't be late. You didn't show up at our agreed time, so we'll have to reschedule," or "I waited as long as I could. Still, I can't wait any longer. I have another commitment," or even, "I can stay this time, but really, I need you to be on time going forward. We can't continue meeting if you don't show up on time."

The Third Scenario: This scenario is a common one for HSPs! Someone is constantly dumping their emotional baggage on you and expecting you to always be there for them for all their needs. Enter narcissist partner. Before, you might have let them go on and on, giving up your time or missing out on things you enjoy because of this. Time to set that boundary!

You can say, "I'm sorry you're going through this, but now is not a good time for me to talk. I have an appointment I'll be late for if I don't leave now!" Or "Now's not a great time, but I'd love to hear about this when I can give you my full attention. Let's talk later!" Or you can even gently remind them of their personal responsibility to seek out the resources they need. "This doesn't sound fun at all. What are you going to do to get the support you need during this time?"

If you are using a pen or highlighter as you read this book, you'll want to underline this next paragraph.

Beware of the contradiction when you speak a boundary but do not follow it up with your actions. After you have clearly communicated your line with words, you need to stay behind it with your behaviour. For example, let's say you are dating someone who calls you at work when you prefer not to be interrupted. You make up your mind and tell your partner in a firm but friendly way you don't want to be disturbed at work, but still answer the phone the next time they call the office. In that scenario, your actions have contradicted your words, even if you answer the phone just to remind them not to call. But if you refuse to pick up the phone, you remain in and hold your territory, and they stay behind the line you requested. This situation has now demonstrated the character of your date and will be a sign to you that they are not worthy of your trust.

People who lack self-discipline, or those who are particularly bold, will not stop trying to take from you once you verbally oppose their actions by communicating your perimeter. Therefore, you must also enforce your boundaries with action so these disrespectful wanderers won't end up in your territory.

Conclusion

Setting boundaries can feel challenging, especially in the beginning. People are likely to react to your sudden boundary-setting. They may not like it or express disappointment or surprise. Their reaction proves they benefitted from your lack of boundaries because they were able to take advantage of you. Don't let that stop you from doing what is healthy. Besides, if someone truly loves and respects you in their lives, they will respect your boundaries. They won't make you feel guilty, or like you're being unreasonable.

This process of boundary creation will take time, but it's the next significant step of recovery on your healing journey. You are building a new life after abuse, and boundaries keep it beautiful.

Summary

This chapter focused on building boundaries in social spaces with your friends, family and co-workers.

- Boundaries are hard to build with others because HSPs are people-pleasers!

- Use your interactions with others to help you figure out where you need to start building boundaries.

- Saying "no" isn't about being mean. It's about taking control of your life and protecting yourself.

- Hold your boundary line and territory by making sure your actions match what you have stated verbally.

Next, we will go deeper into the topic of boundaries by examining what it means to "hold space" for ourselves.

Holding Space for Yourself

WHEN WE HIGHLY SENSITIVE people spend time in the presence of others, we feel their emotions. We sense their discomfort, their happiness, their sadness, or even their anger. We are not mind-readers, but we can feel the energy they give off, and we have the desire to help them feel better if they're feeling down. We want to be present for people, especially those we love, so we hold a space for them in our lives. Think of your best friend or your sibling. This person is dear to your heart, so you always have a place for them to come and share with you, be themselves with you, and come to you in any sort of mood.

That's why it's so exhausting being an HSP. We sometimes do this with strangers or mere acquaintances! While this is a beautiful aspect of being highly sensitive, I want to focus on this idea: you also need to hold space for yourself. Let me be clear. I'm not simply referring to your daily commitment to entering your sacred space to rest and let yourself be. That's part of it, sure, but this is more about holding a space for yourself in life just as much as you hold a space for others. It's about getting out of your own way and giving yourself the full, rich life you deserve.

What Does Holding Space Mean?

Holding space is kind of a vague, psychological concept. But essentially, it means just what it says. It's about intentionally creating space that can be filled with something. For yourself, it's about leaving room to live just as you want to live, and it's about giving space for others to join you on your journey.

Once I had left everything familiar that tied me to my narcissist ex, I felt extremely uncomfortable with the vacancies of my life. When I moved into my own home in a new neighbourhood and my children were away for the weekends to visit their father, the emptiness and silence felt unbearable. In the void, I felt broken, abandoned, and lonely. At first, I would avoid the echoes by leaving the house. I drove an hour to spend weekends overnight with my parents or took the spare room at a friend's house in a nearby town. But eventually, I decided I needed to occupy my own space. Sure, I still left the house to go for walks, visit friends, and go to church, but I started spending more time alone at home and was determined to change my mindset. I enrolled in an online course. I threw myself into developing my skillset and creating a new reality for myself. I made friends with my neighbours. I wrote and published my first book. I began a second business. I dreamed of all the possibilities and stopped accepting the pain of my life as the endpoint. I chose instead to recognize and accept the emptiness for what it truly represented: space to grow.

Holding space for yourself to grow means getting out of your own way so you can create a world for yourself just the way you want it to be. You will need to face your feelings and challenges head-on. Not unlike when you hold space for someone else so they can express and experience and move through their emotions, you will have to allow and sit in the discomfort of all your feelings of inadequacy. You will need to stop running away from your reality and come out of hiding. There are two parts to this. First, you need to create the space for yourself (more boundary building!), and second, you need to hold the space (boundary keeping!) The creation will likely be easier than the holding, but let me get you started with a few examples (Schroeder, n.d.).

10 Ways to Create and Hold Space for Yourself

Be intentional and organized about your time: As an HSP, having control over my time is very important. It helps to reduce a lot of anxiety and overloading of sensitivity when I'm intentional about my time management. When you take control of this area instead of letting others do it for you, you are both establishing a boundary and holding a space for yourself to do what makes you happy. Being intentional about your time also means not wasting it by watching Netflix or sleeping the day away because it's less effort and the path of least resistance. Don't sleep longer than necessary and set boundaries for yourself around mindless leisure activities; instead of spending time, invest your time by forming good habits that align with your goals.

Be committed to your dreams: So often, we let our dreams fall by the wayside because we're so exhausted from living in a crazy, emotion-evoking world or from helping other people, and we forget to serve ourselves in this way. Taking steps toward dreams or goals can be frightening for us. Conflict might arise; we might not achieve what we want or realize something negative about ourselves. Those emotions and situations are heavy for HSPs to digest, so it's not uncommon for HSPs to abandon their dreams and goals. But it's time to stop that. Hold space for yourself and put a boundary between you and whatever's holding you back from committing to your dreams. Start doing what scares you to make you better or to lead you closer to what you truly want.

Take a step back from social media: Everyday life and routine interactions with other humans can be draining enough for an HSP. Add social media on top of that, and it's just begging for trouble and overstimulation. Maybe it's time to break from the extra stress. You might notice a great relief. By reining in the time spent on shows, movies and social media, you have more energy to give yourself. You're holding space for yourself and creating the potential for more in your daily life.

Start putting yourself first: I know this sounds crazy! But when you hold space for yourself, it means putting yourself first. This is not a bad thing. I repeat: this is not a bad thing. I don't think we have to worry about HSPs ever going overboard with putting themselves first, so you shouldn't worry about it yourself. Try little ways to put yourself first, such as saying "no" when you want to. Then, build up to the bigger things.

Face your fears: With the heightened ability to feel comes the acuteness of fear in an HSP's life. But when you hide from what scares you, you're letting the fear control your life instead of maintaining your authority. Hold space for yourself and face your fears. Work through your uncomfortable feelings. Set a boundary with the fear and stop it from keeping you from living fully.

Think about therapy or an HSP support group: Give yourself the space to be yourself by not avoiding your high sensitivity and working with it. Therapy can help you work through the history with your abuser as well as help you deal with your heightened sensitivity day to day. You can learn to celebrate it and enjoy life with it. Provide yourself with the support you need as an HSP in a non-HSP world.

Plan a weekly date with yourself: This differs from your daily sacred space practice. For this date, why not spend time journaling and getting things out you might not have had a chance to express during the week? This provides space for you to unpack and evaluate those emotions you have. The chatter in your mind can be relieved when you write your thoughts on paper. Your mind and heart will be swept and tidied with room for other things to take up your time, and you will also feel rested and fulfilled.

Spend more time outside: Time in nature can help ease anxiety and fear, creating a sense of peace and calm. HSPs know this! Take some time out of your day to spend in nature. Go for a walk. Read on a park bench. Watch the birds. Admire some flowers. Find a waterfront. Whatever it is, get out and commune with nature. Let yourself feel and be out in the open world all on your own. It's your chance to be you without any external stressors or judgment.

Cut the comparison: Comparing yourself and your abilities or progress to others will only bring misery. You are a unique person! You have such special gifts to offer the world and yourself! We are all on our own journeys, so keep your eyes focused straight ahead. By comparing, you're limiting the space and freedom you give yourself. You're trying to be more like somebody else instead of enjoying who you are.

Stop rescuing others: It's time to leave people to the consequences of their actions and to separate yourself from their needs. HSPs are often guilty of coming to the rescue and saving people who could perfectly save themselves. I have certainly been guilty of investing in and being more committed to someone's potential than they were. It steals much-needed energy from ourselves, leaving us feeling drained and exhausted. Think about where you've been helping others too much, and take a step back. Let people handle their own lives. We are all in control of our own actions. Your rescue attempts are likely hindering that person from taking responsibility for their behaviours. Consequences redirect us when we get off track. When you intercept someone else's consequences, eating the rotten fruit of their poor decisions, you shelter them from the redirecting pain of the consequence and enable them to continue on the wrong path. More than co-dependent, this way of living is hypocritical. Your investment into someone else comes at the expense of your own potential. Stop dimming your light so others can shine. The more you separate from others, the better you can create and expand your world and unique identity.

These actions are part of what it means to hold space for yourself.

Boundary Maintenance

When you hold space for yourself, you surpass ordinary boundary-setting. You are not simply patrolling your perimeter, monitoring wrong behaviour; you are paving the runway to your next level. In fact, holding space is the outward expansion of your borders so that you occupy more territory. So, hold fast to the practice of giving yourself space and room to grow into the marvellous creature God designed you to be, to live the life you deserve to the fullest.

Building boundaries is one thing. Keeping them intact is entirely another. One way you can do this is to write down the boundaries you've decided. You can make a list or procure a physical reminder to cue you to identify the boundary and remember it. It might be something you want to carry in your pocket to remind yourself when you get into certain situations. Boundary maintenance can also be assisted through therapy or group support. When someone else helps you establish your boundaries, you have accountability for being consistent. You may falter occasionally, but that's okay. We're only human. The more you maintain your boundaries, the more confident you'll become, and the easier it will be to hold fast to them.

Conclusion

As HSPs and victims of narcissistic abuse, I want us to remember how to love and show up for ourselves. Our abusive partners broke our sense of identity. It can feel like we're roaming around in a dark, uncertain world, feeling deeply but unsure how to channel those intense feelings in a healthy and productive way. Holding space and creating boundaries with yourself (and others) is a wonderful way to love and appreciate who you are as an HSP. This is the way to build a life you never thought possible in a world that seemed to reject you. Holding space for yourself is remaining a part of the world while creating your own cozy universe inside it, one in which you are loved, appreciated, and found worthy of all the good things you receive.

Summary

This chapter focuses on holding space for yourself.

- Holding space is about getting out of your own way to live a whole and beautiful life as an HSP.

- It's about facing all the uncomfortable feelings and reframing loss as potential.

- Give yourself the space to be who you are and work with your high sensitivity instead of against it.

- Holding space means creating boundaries with yourself and others. This is an expression of loving and honouring yourself.

In the final chapter, I want to hone in on your physical spaces and how you can create and build a physical environment which serves you well.

Part Five: Clear The Clutter

Simplicity and Slowness in Physical Spaces

YOU KNOW THE PHRASE, "you are what you eat"? Well, I'd like to propose "you are where you live." I am referring to your environment and the possessions you surround yourself with. Although our physical habitat is entirely separate from our bodies, it still severely affects us, especially as HSPs. If you don't believe me, then imagine yourself in a forest. It's vibrant green and calm; the muted light filters through the leaves, and all you can hear is the gentle breeze and the calling of birds. Then suddenly, you're switched to a busy, fluorescent office space. Everyone's in a frenzy, answering phones, typing emails, and rushing to and from meetings. There's a constant humming sound from the whirring printers and copiers, ringing phones, and chatting colleagues.

How do you feel in each space? Did you go from calm and at peace to stressed and anxious? The physical space around an HSP has a significant impact on their well-being. Therefore, HSPs must strategically position themselves and their environments to support their sensitivities. Minimalism, slow living, and time in nature are all effective strategies to promote calm and create a sanctuary for HSPs.

Why This Effect on Us?

What aspects of our physical, non-natural environments can distract us, change our moods, and affect us in many ways? First off, the noise level has a considerable effect. Ever tried to write or enjoy a cup of coffee in a cafe when it was blasting music? It's nearly impossible. We HSPs are so "tuned in" to everything around us that if one aspect of the environment becomes more potent than the rest, we focus on it. As a result, all our energy goes there instead of where it needs to be. In the physical spaces you find yourself, work to minimize the noise level or find ways around it, such as noise-cancelling headphones. You know yourself and what you need to be at your best.

For some HSPs, lighting is a big issue. This is the case for a lot of non-HSPs as well. Just think about the moment in sci-fi TV shows where they want you to feel nervous and on edge. You get that weird, bright science-y lighting in the scene, and it creates the corresponding emotion: tension, uncertainty, and anxiety. Not exactly what an HSP needs in her life. Try to moderate lighting to a degree where you feel comfortable in your physical spaces. If you work in an office where the lighting is distracting or affecting you negatively, see if you can make a change by explaining to your supervisor how it could improve your work efficiency. One day after the bright luminary burned out in my kitchen fixture, I replaced it with the only spare I had on hand, a single, warm-toned 60-watt bulb. Though non-HSP visitors tell me it is too dark in that space, I find the soft, warm glow cozy and such a relief from the previous brightness which was harsh on my eyes. I supplement with similar soft-toned under-the-cabinet lighting when prepping food, and this is just right for me.

Dear HSP, you tie so many outward things to your inner world. Simply the physical placement of yourself in a room can affect you significantly. For example, some people dislike turning their back toward an open area because it makes them uncomfortable. The same goes for HSPs who are stuffed into a corner. It might make them feel trapped or claustrophobic. So be mindful to discover what makes you most comfortable in a space. Where do you like to sit, and what part of the room makes you happiest and most effective?

The height of a room causes certain HSPs to feel comfortable or uncomfortable. Some prefer low ceilings for those cozy moments. Imagine an old pub on a winter's day with a roaring fire in the hearth. On the other hand, that could make some HSPs feel suffocated or trapped. Some prefer higher ceilings, such as cathedral style, especially for creative tasks like writing. But for others, the vast openness could make them feel like there is too much space and they are overexposed. Since you likely have limited control in your workplace, spend your free time where you feel at ease and can relax, such as in a room of your house or space in another building like a cafe (Stephanides, 2021).

Some HSPs, like myself, prefer to work from home because we control our physical space. However, if that is not an option for you, and your office space is less than ideal, you can find other ways to enjoy physical spaces which bring you peace and joy. Enter the natural world.

Time in Nature

While many are drawn to the outside world and excited to spend time there, highly sensitive people are more apt to feel this way. Just like we can feel the energy of the people who surround us each day, we feel the vital energy of the natural world when we enter it. Only this time, the sounds and vibrations of nature are much more soothing. The outside world is free from the constant buzz of humanity, the eternally-moving machine of the extroverted, non-HSP world. Many HSPs believe nature gives them a place of escape, a home away from home, and if you have not taken advantage of this, it's time to start!

They say time heals all wounds, but nature is a healing balm on them as well. Studies show only 20 minutes out in nature can do wonders for lifting the mood (Messerschmidt, 2016). As you well know, highly sensitive people need alone time to take a break from the intensity of the world, and nature is a great place to rest. It could simply be a walk through the park, a small hike through the forest, or sitting by a peaceful body of water. So, find ways to get out into the natural world to find your peace and take a breath.

What exactly can nature do for an HSP like you? First, spending time outside can act as a therapist: I sometimes treat green space like a therapist because just walking (or driving!) through and enjoying it heals my soul. It gives me the time and space to work through some inner emotions or thoughts I haven't yet had time to ponder. It's almost like I'm sharing energy with the nature around me, letting go of what's not serving me and taking on what will rejuvenate me.

Second, time in nature can act as a creative space. Nature often inspires people to do something creative such as writing or painting. While you're spending time in nature, consider something like journaling to express how you feel in the moment. It's also a chance to get things out while you're feeling the restorative power of nature's presence, and it can really help to bring about a sense of calm.

Spending time in nature can also help you connect to your spiritual side. Spirituality isn't necessarily tied to religion. There's nothing like standing alone in the dark looking up at a million trillion stars while the Northern Lights dance green and pink across the sky. Even if you're not religious, you can still enjoy the energy of natural space and how it makes you feel small in front of its awe-inspiring views. Likewise, admiring nature's intricacies and petite beauties can give us a break from ourselves and take us away for a while, providing us with the rest we need (Messerschmidt, 2016).

Time in nature can partner neatly with exercise. Part of living a healthy life is taking care of your body. Highly sensitive people need to take special care of their bodies because our physical and emotional selves are so tied together. I know I always feel better when I'm consistent with my exercise, and I love it when I can connect my physical activity with time spent in nature. So, kill two birds with one stone, as they say, and jump out into nature while exercising. Walking, hiking, swimming, etc., are great ways to benefit simultaneously from exercise and nature.

Spending time in natural spaces can give you strength. I find time in nature silences both the voices of the world and the voices in my head. It's a place where I can regain the strength I've given away to others in my busy day. In nature, I can just relax because I'm no longer worried about people pleasing or having to read anyone's emotions. I can just be and settle in and enjoy what surrounds me. This quiet time not only gives me strength, but it helps to remind me who I am and that I am deserving of love.

How Else Can I Control My Physical Space?

Another brilliant and effective way you can create calming and pleasurable physical spaces is to subscribe to the idea of minimalism! A hot topic these days, minimalism could be an excellent bandwagon for highly sensitive people to board. Minimalism is decluttering your home to declutter your life. There are many ways to apply minimalism, such as minimal meal planning or minimizing your electronic files, but let's focus on physical spaces.

HSPs can benefit from a life of material minimalism. The world doesn't cater to us, so it's pleasant and a relief when we can return to our home after a long, hard day to an ordered and calm sanctuary. Look around your house. When you come into your home each day, does it make you stressed and anxious, or do you feel calm and relaxed? If piles, excess and disorder abound, consider slowly and methodically reducing the clutter you've built up in your house (*Why highly sensitive people need minimalism*, 2021).

The physical act of doing this can be cathartic and cleansing for highly sensitive people. Since we tend to hold onto emotions, thoughts and ideals when they no longer serve us, the physical act of letting something go can teach us how to do the same in the parallel places of our minds and hearts. Going through your possessions allows you to reflect on your life, how your space works for you and what truly makes you happy. If it's a practical item, have you used it in the last year? If it's sentimental or decorative, do you love it? If your stuff brings you happiness and positivity, keep it. But if you don't use it and it offers something negative or nothing at all, give it away.

As you go through each item, think about what message it is communicating. For example, clothes in the back of our closet that don't fit us properly may express that we are failing in our ideals of losing weight. Tools left in the corner can nag us about a project we have neglected. Jewellery or gifts from our ex may remind us of that person and the pain they caused us. Tidying up and intentionally removing items by donating, throwing them out, or even having a garage sale can silence all the "noise."

Minimalism is about reducing your clutter and the negative messages it communicates to you. As a result, you will quiet down your house, minimizing your stress and tension. It is also much simpler to clean and maintain a spacious home with fewer possessions. As an HSP, you need a sanctuary. Your home can become one if you embrace the simplicity of having only the things you use regularly and enjoy. I would highly suggest it, especially at this delicate time of recovery.

I love that every room in my home is spacious, uncluttered and beautiful, filled with things I have positive associations with and love. By thrifting and accepting unused furniture from friends and family, I replaced most items from my past life so my possessions would not trigger any painful memories. When I think about my stuff, I remember the kindness of friends and family who supported my transition into a better life because of the furniture and goods they helped me acquire.

Slow Living: What's This?

I noticed a remarkable change of pace when I moved to the city as a young adult. The time and effort to navigate six lanes of traffic to get to a grocery store that was as big as the mall in my hometown was exhausting! Previously, it was a 2-minute drive to "downtown," where there were only two food stores to choose from, and they were a street apart. I could walk to my office on the waterfront when I lived in a small rural town, but when I embraced urban life, I drove 35 minutes or longer in rush hour traffic to get to work. I still live in an urban environment, but I have recently decided to return to and foster the mindset of a slower-paced life.

You may not be aware of the concept or option that is "slow living." This movement originated in Italy during the 1980s and began when a popular fast-food franchise opened in Rome. Carlo Petrini and other activists merged to respond by celebrating and preserving the local "slow food" tradition. Celebrating slowness is now an art and a movement for multitudes and is continuing to gain international momentum, experiencing a recent hike in popularity since the global events of 2020 when society everywhere came to a standstill. During lockdowns and extended time at home, people finally realized what they were missing out on.

Well over 3 million people have viewed a TED talk by Journalist Carl Honoré, who wrote the book, *In Praise of Slowness*. After Honoré noticed himself speeding up and racing through his evening ritual of reading bedtime stories to his son, he took a step back to examine his life and priorities. Asking, "how did the world get so fast?" and, "is it possible or even desirable to slow down?" he decided to investigate the idea of slow living. What he discovered was a counter-cultural mindset to that of Western society, where "time is money". In other countries, locals embrace a slower, more intentional pace of life, including a 35-hour workweek and a calendar with few scheduled extra-curricular activities for their kids. The result is an experience of better health, work, relationships and quality of life for adults and children alike. So, Honoré reformed his habits and embraced living his life instead of racing through it. He reports the same result: better quality of life and richer, more profound and meaningful relationships, including with his son, who has since praised him as "the best story-reader in the world."

Our society is not about taking things slow, and it's tough for HSPs (and very draining!) to keep up. But we don't have to. Slow living is figuring out where you can pump the brakes in your life to get the most out of an experience. Highly sensitive people have such a unique perspective on the world. It is a shame to waste it by rushing through life, skimming the surface of experiences and coming back with only an exhausted body and mind to show for it.

Slow living is cutting out distracting activities such as social media or too much TV. It's prioritizing what is most important to you: reducing draining activities such as too many nights out, a long commute etc. Slow living is also spending time on things that bring you joy instead of rushing through everything and checking it off a list (*What is slow living?* n.d.).

Doesn't this sound ideal for an HSP? We want the time to do things we love, but it's rare to have and take that time. Instead, we find ourselves distracted by other people and noise and busyness. As you recover from the abuse you experienced, slow down, and contemplate. Your future, which might seem bleak and dark now, can become bright again, especially as you embrace a more intentional and simplified way of life.

Conclusion

The world is a wild, hectic place on its own, and it's even more of a frenzy for an HSP who doesn't understand how they can work with their unique personality. Getting back control through time management and adjusting your physical spaces can bring stability, balance, and an atmosphere conducive to healing. Understanding how you react to your physical surroundings also teaches you more about yourself.

Highly sensitive people are often too busy and too distracted, neglecting themselves. Abuse makes this even worse. When you're pumped out on the other side of a breakup with a narcissistic abuser, you have no idea who you are or what makes you tick. But creating a sanctuary space for your escape can help you remember who you are or help you discover yourself for the first time. Make your physical spaces work for you; consider decluttering your life through minimalism and ponder how you can approach life with a slow-living mindset. These are great ways to take control of your life as a highly sensitive person.

Summary

I discussed how physical surroundings and spaces affect highly sensitive people in this chapter.

- Our physical surroundings absolutely have an emotional effect on us.
- Whether it's noise, ceiling height, or clutter, we need to figure out what we need from our physical environments to make us feel more focused and less overwhelmed.

- Minimalism and slow living give HSPs more peace and control over their lives and spaces.

Your journey to understanding yourself will continue, as will your healing. Recovery is in your hands now. Build the world in which you want to live and always make a forward motion toward the life you desire and deserve.

Final Words

I congratulate you on taking the initiative to heal and regain control over your life by reading this book. Abuse, especially narcissistic abuse, is a horrific and unfortunate aspect of many highly sensitive people's lives. But the hazardous correlation between narcs and HSPs doesn't mean you deserved the mistreatment or that you are weak or useless as your abuser tried to convince you. It merely implies a narcissist found you and chose to abuse you, just like Derrick and Tabitha. Unfortunately, Tabitha fell into the narcissist trap Derrick set for her, and she became a victim of his insidious emotional and mental abuse. But her story wasn't sad or pathetic in the end, and it won't be for you either. Your history will declare empowerment, hope, and freedom. In the end, Tabitha broke free from Derrick, her abuser, and she left behind the chains that kept her from sharing her beautiful gifts with the world and herself.

Now is your chance to do the same. Whether you're still with your abusive narcissist partner or have recently made a plan and decision to part ways, you can benefit from all we have discussed. It is my hope and aspiration, through sharing these tools and strategies, for highly sensitive people everywhere to realize their unique personhood and appreciate its sacredness. Everyone deserves love, acceptance and to feel worthy of something/someone; HSPs are no different. My intention is to give you the strength you need to build yourself up so you can be a compassionate person who loves yourself, follows your dreams, and uses your unique strengths to your advantage.

Even though you are different from non-HSPs and need time away in your sanctuary, I don't want you to feel entirely separate from the world. Yes, you are your own person and must carve out your independence and identity, but you are still human. Being an HSP doesn't mean you have nothing to share with non-HSPs. We all share the ordinary, everyday experiences of life.

While I encourage you to put yourself first and release the bonds of toxic relationships, I also encourage you to seek connection and communion with others.

Especially immediately after coming out of your abuse, you need the support of other loving, non-toxic people as you make your journey forward. Others can help you build your boundaries, encourage you to follow your dreams, and provide a gentle, cheerful voice to counter the harsh and demeaning messages planted in your mind by the narcissist. There is beauty in being alone, but, as my mentor told me, don't be an island. Don't take it too far and isolate yourself by refusing to be vulnerable. I know you've been hurt, and it can feel dangerous and uncomfortable to return to the world again.

However, it is not friendship or romantic relationships that are wrong. It is the abuse you suffered at the hands of your narcissistic partner. They were counterfeit, twisting the beautiful gifts you have as a highly sensitive person until you believed these gifts made you strange or weak. The truth is your gifts give you strength. HSPs have the power to live extraordinary lives if we learn how to work strategically with our sensitivity instead of against it.

Before I leave you, these truths need to get into your head and become embedded in you as you put one foot in front of the other on your adventure to a better life. Return to these as often as possible, especially when you hear the voice of your abuser in your head trying to drown out the positive things you want to believe about yourself:

- "I am deserving of friendship."
- "I am worthy of love."
- "There are high-quality individuals who would enjoy being my friend or partner."
- "I have the capacity to be a good friend and partner."

Remember also, that every person needs a safe space to be authentic, to feel all emotions without judgment and rest from the world's craziness, to establish separateness and independence from others, and enjoy their unique personhood.

After you free yourself from the abuse of your narcissist partner, it may feel like you've just been reborn, and you're taking your first wobbly steps into the world. Everything is new and strange. You may feel a sense of loneliness after you've cut ties with your partner and the people who connect you to their toxicity. I was there once, and even though my first steps were rickety, they still moved me forward so I could gain the strength needed to create the life I always wanted. Keep in mind that there is no particular destination; it's all about the adventure of the journey.

The future is at hand. High sensitivity is not a disease or a disorder. It's something unique, so do not drown it out or diminish it. Dear HSP, stand proud. Give to others, experience a more profound life, and most of all, give compassion, kindness, and love to yourself day after day. It will make all the difference.

Afterword

You now have the tools and knowledge I used to come through the most difficult season of my entire life. But for all its merits this book falls short of giving you the most powerful Resource that impacted my recovery journey. I did not find this road on my own. I was not alone and you don't have to be either. I have shown you a recovery path and now I would like to introduce you to the Way.

Jesus answered, "I am the way and the truth and the life..." John 14:6

www.christianityexplored.org

Leave a Review!

REVIEWS GO A LONG way in getting this book into the hands of other recovering highly sensitive souls who will truly benefit from the strategies and truths outlined in this book. I would be absolutely grateful for your honest feedback about *Narcissistic Abuse Recovery* over at your local Amazon store.

Review on Amazon.com

Review on Amazon.co.uk

Review on Amazon.ca

Join A Supportive Community!

Would you like to join a supportive community of highly sensitive people recovering from narcissistic abuse together? We'd love to have you in our Facebook group! Find us at: www.facebook.com/groups/thehighlysensitivepersonsrecovery

My Gift to You

Hello Lovely! I have put together a 33-page companion workbook to go along with the many practical strategies described in *Narcissistic Abuse Recovery*. Grab your free PDF copy, print it out and refer to it as you continue reading. I think it will be a great additional resource for your healing journey!

Grab it here! freebie.myrecoveryyear.com

Cheers to your recovery!

Loralee Jean

LORALEE JEAN

NARCISSTIC ABUSE

15-Minute Activities and Reflections
For a New Life of Beauty & Peace

References

@dealwithnarcissist. (2020, June 10). *Exploring mindfulness and narcissistic abuse: can mindfulness be helpful when dealing with narcissists?* Deal With Narcissist.

10 signs of an unhealthy relationship. (n.d.). One Love Foundation.

Andersen, N. (2018, July 23). *20 self-care ideas for highly sensitive people.* Highly Sensitive Refuge.

Arabi, S. (2017, May 1). *30 kickass affirmations for going no contact with an abusive narcissist.* Thought Catalog.

Aron, E. (2013, May 13). *Introversion, extroversion, and the highly sensitive person.* Psychology Today.

Atkinson, A. (n.d.). *Narcissistic abuse recovery guided meditation for self-acceptance and self-love*. Queen Beeing.

Brogaard, B. (2019, June 23). *Vulnerable vs grandiose narcissism: Which is more harmful?* Psychology Today.

Business Made Simple. (2019, May 6). *This trick instantly cures confusion* [Video]. YouTube.

Cherry, K. (2021b, April 29). *What is a mindset and why it matters*. Verywell Mind.

Cherry, K. (2022, July 28). *Myers-Briggs type indicator: The 16 personality types*. Verywell Mind.

Demartini, Dr. J. (2020, July 2). *How To Determine Your Core Values | 13 Questions with Dr John Demartini*. [Video]. YouTube.

denmarkguy. (2020, May 25). *HSPs and self-care: Putting yourself first is not selfish*. Sensitive Evolution.

Granneman, J. (2017, May 8). *23 signs that you're a highly sensitive person*. Introvert, Dear.

Hardman, J. (n.d.). *How to set boundaries as a highly sensitive person – with scripts!* Josephine Hardman, PhD.

Honoré, C. (2007, February 28). *In praise of slowness* [Video]. TED Talks.

Jarai, M. (2022, February 11). *What is a highly sensitive person?* Medical News Today.

Jas @ INF club. (2019, September 11). *An HSP & Myers-Briggs mini-study.* INF Club.

M. (n.d.). *Highly sensitive or sensory processing disorder?* The Highly Sensitive Child.

Mackenzie-Smith, K. (2022, January 29). *How to actually set better boundaries as a highly sensitive person.* Highly Sensitive Refuge.

McMahan, J. (2017, August 14). *Boundaries and relationships: How secure limits help build better trust.* Janie McMahan.

Messerschmidt, P. (2016, September 6). *HSP living: The highly sensitive person and the healing power of nature.* HubPages.

Miller, L. (n.d.). *The highly-sensitive person (HSP) and narcissistic abuse. 7 tips to self-protect.* Narcissist Abuse Support.

Orloff, J. (2017, June 3). *The differences between highly sensitive people and empaths.* Psychology Today.

Parker, L. (2021, October 13). *10 signs you're in a healthy relationship as an HSP.* Highly Sensitive Refuge.

Penney, R. (2018, November 21). *Reframing boundaries the HSP way.* Hspworld.

Samson, R. (2021, December 7). *No, being autistic is not the same as being highly sensitive.* Psychology Today.

Schroeder, A. (n.d.). *25 ways to hold space for yourself (and your dreams).* Creative Dream Incubator.

Selig, M. (2018, November 4). *6 ways to discover and choose your core values.* Psychology Today.

Steber, C. (2021, May 18). *21 questions that can help you find clarity in your relationship.* Bustle.

Stephanides, E. (2021, December 20). *Why a little bit of environmental psychology can be life-changing for HSPs.* Highly Sensitive Refuge.

Talks at Google. (2019, November 8). *Understanding the highly sensitive person | Alane Freund | Talks at Google* [Video]. YouTube.

Taylor, J. (n.d.). *Are you a highly sensitive person? Maybe the DOES acronym can help you decide!* Habits for Wellbeing.

Valko, L. (2020, November 29). *How to create your own HSP sanctuary.* Highly Sensitive Refuge.

Vogel, K. (2022, July 14). *Making friends as an adult isn't easy, so we came up with 102 expert-backed ways to do it.* Parade.

Ward, D. (2012, January 16). *The highly sensitive person and the narcissist.* Psychology Today.

Ward, D. (2017, January 2). *Are all INFJs highly sensitive people?* Truity.

What is slow living? (n.d.). Slow Living LDN.

Why highly sensitive people need minimalism. (2021, April 20). Becoming UnBusy.

www.ingramcontent.com/pod-product-compliance
Lightning Source LLC
Chambersburg PA
CBHW072051110526
44590CB00018B/3119